JOURNEY'S END

CA KIRKHAM

ILLUMIFY MEDIA GLOBAL
Littleton, Colorado

Published by
Illumify Media Global
www.IllumifyMedia.com
"We bring your book to life!"

Library of Congress Control Number: 2020921257

Paperback ISBN: 978-1-947360-76-1
eBook ISBN: 978-1-947360-77-8

Cover design by Debbie Lewis

Printed in the United States of America

For Mom, who has always encouraged me
to write a book,
and for Jared, who I hope will one day read a book: especially
mine.

I would like to thank my lovely wife for giving me the space and time to write.

"The Lord, a merciful and gracious God, slow to anger and rich in kindness and fidelity, continuing his kindness for a thousand generations, and forgiving wickedness, crime and sin; yet not declaring the guilty guiltless, but punishing the children and grandchildren to the third and fourth generation for their fathers' wickedness."

Exodus 34:6–7

"If a man begets a son who, seeing all the sins his father commits yet fears and does not imitate them. . . this one shall not die for the sins of the father, but shall surely live."

Ezekiel 18:14–17

CHAPTER ONE

As sunlight shone through the bedroom windows, I awoke to the local news blaring on the TV. "Early this morning a high–speed police chase ended when three men crashed a stolen car into a Lakewood hamburger stand. After receiving an anonymous tip, Denver Police were pursuing the suspects as they fired shots at officers," said the news reporter.

As I looked around, I felt hollow inside and groggy from a fitful night of sleep. The blaring TV, which now irritated me with people babbling in loud, animated voices was left on last night out of my fear of ghosts. The encounter with a spirit in my backyard last night left me afraid to be alone, and the TV noise soothed my anxiety.

I twisted my body sideways and grabbed the remote from the nightstand and switched the TV off. As silence immediately flooded the room, I rolled onto my back and pushed my head deeper into a pillow. I stared at the ceiling fan rotating above me and replayed events in my mind.

My fiancée Sophia and I got into a heated argument

yesterday when she started talking about her desire to have two children, a boy and a girl. The idea of children has always scared me, as I'm terrified that I would end up breaking them or screwing up their lives. Kids are too fragile, and my bloodlines run deep with addictions and family secrets. Having children would be like cracking the screen door and hoping a fly doesn't make it into the house. What inevitably happens? A fly gets into the house, and you spend ten minutes chasing it around with a fly swatter trying to eliminate it. With my luck, drug addiction would seep into my kids, and I'd spend my life chasing it, trying to eliminate it.

Sophia wouldn't let the issue go. Even after I told her about my brother Tommy, she was insistent that I wouldn't screw up the kids because my desire to reject addictions was greater than genetics. Maybe she was right, but I just couldn't risk it. Sophia was far more optimistic than I could ever be. The oozing blackness of addiction had periodically crept into my life even though I had consciously chosen to be different from my dad, different from my family, different from what everyone expected. While I was growing up, I always heard the silent whispers of extended family members, saying, "Wild George's son surely will become crazy James." But I didn't and I wouldn't. I left that circus life as far behind as I could. I started running before the gun went off. And now Sophia wants to set up colorful tents adorned with caged animals and clowns.

We fought until we were both too tired to fight. When our conversation ended with resigned silence, I got up and left her apartment, unsure if we were still getting married or not. Sophia was my soul mate and I could not imagine life without her, but the thought of children frightened me.

When I arrived at my 1950s–style tan brick home in

south Denver, I threw my keys on the counter, opened the refrigerator, and grabbed a cold Miller Lite. My answering machine was flashing red. I had a message to call my sister Jennifer as soon as possible. I immediately dialed her number, and she sobbed into the phone that our Dad was found dead in a motel room. I was shocked but without emotion. In an eerie way, I expected the call.

He had called three days ago and said he was packing up his stuff and driving back to Denver. He was wasted, and with his penchant for drunk driving I was expecting that he would fatally wreck his car.

A pang of guilt washed over me when Jennifer called. I didn't want my dad to come back and had been dreading it ever since he called. His arrival was sure to bring chaos with him. Life had been quiet since he moved to Orlando, Florida and I just couldn't face the non–stop problems that his lifestyle generated. But I never wanted this to happen! No matter how much I prepared myself for this moment, I still wasn't prepared. I longed for a relationship with him, and the realization that he was gone tore at my heart.

After hanging up the phone with Jennifer I twisted the bottle cap off and took a long swig from the bottle of beer. Forcefully exhaling my inner turmoil, I walked out the back door, throwing the cap in the trash on my way out.

As I stepped onto my porch, I could see orange and purple clouds stretched across the sky as the sun slid behind the distant mountains. A warm, late summer breeze blew against my face and tree leaves whooshed while I walked across the porch to my plastic chair butted up against the back of the house. When I sat down, my body felt heavy and depleted of energy. I took another swig of beer and thought about Sophia, wondering how I'd fix things. When my mind exhausted thoughts of

Sophia, I wondered what happened to my dad in the motel room.

Lying on my back and lost in my thoughts, I was thankful for the daylight. My mind was still trying to process events as I recounted them:

When I finished my beer, the sky had become dark with the glow of city lights rising against it. Yellow light from my kitchen poured out of the window casting shadows on the porch. As the warm air breezed, rustling the thick canopy of tree leaves in my backyard, I began to sense something sinister, like a spirit was standing in front of me, trying to communicate something. As the peculiar feeling wafted over me, I became mesmerized by the two apple trees in my backyard. It was as if the trees were intelligent lifeforms standing in the yard, waving their arms, and yelling at me.

In an attempt to shake the bizarre feeling, I got up and walked into the house for a second beer. As I stepped into the kitchen, the yellow light hurt my eyes while they adjusted from the darkness. I threw the empty bottle in the trash and walked across the kitchen to the refrigerator. I opened the door and retrieved another bottle of beer. This would be my last one. When I decided to make big changes in my life, one of them was to stop at two beers.

While I twisted off the bottle cap, I suddenly had a strange desire to play a Billy Squier album because my dad would want to hear that if he were hanging out with me. Heeding the urge, I walked across my living room to the tall CD rack in the corner. After a few minutes of searching, I found the Billy Squier CD and played it on the stereo. Thinking about my dad, I cranked up the volume loud enough to hear it on the patio and walked back outside. I felt like he and I were hanging out and enjoying the summer night with a cold beer.

For some reason, I didn't want to sit down on the porch. Instead, I stood on the sidewalk that ended in the middle of the yard. It was a left over from a bygone era of backyard trash incinerators. The trash incinerator had long ago been removed and thick grass grew in its place. Some people converted the incinerators into flower planters, but the previous owners of my house apparently discarded it and planted grass.

As I listened to Billy Squier's songs, the tree branches swayed in the night air while I thought of my dad, imagining conversations with him. I remembered a late spring night when I was in college and we stood outside his duplex listening to a Black Sabbath album smoking cigarettes, drinking beer, and talking loudly about how unique Ozzy Osborne's voice was and how the song lyrics were deeply philosophical.

Strangely, I wanted a cigarette as I stood on the sidewalk reminiscing, but I'd swore the cancer sticks off shortly after I graduated from college. They were one of the many bad habits that seeped into my life during college that I now willfully rejected.

Lost in old thoughts of drinking beer with my dad, I suddenly became creeped out when an imaginary dark form stood in front of me. A smell of rotted flesh wafted into my nostrils causing a sensation of evil darkness covering my brain. I didn't know what it was, but I also had a peculiar feeling it was trying to talk to me. Physically blind to what was happening, I turned and quickly walked into my house, retreating from the summer night as fast as I could.

I was again assaulted by the yellow kitchen lights as I

entered the house. The strange feeling followed me as I walked into my living room and turned the stereo off. The instant silence unnerved me even more as I creepily sensed the ghost from my backyard standing near me. I walked over to my recliner and grabbed the remote resting on the arm and switched the TV on for some white noise. Comforted by the familiar sounds of people talking, I walked into the kitchen and poured the rest of my beer out. I felt creeped out, and the beer no longer appealed to me. I walked back into the living room and sat in my recliner and watched TV, attempting to free my mind from ghostly thoughts.

But I couldn't shake the feeling of the ghostly presence in my backyard. Was Dad visiting me? Can a spirit come back after death?

CHAPTER TWO

While I lay on my bed staring at the ceiling fan, my eyes focused on the blades, following them round and round. I heard birds chirping outside my bedroom windows and felt the cool morning air wafting in. The temperature was already rising, and I would soon have to close all the windows, darken the shades, and turn the swamp cooler on.

I slowly rolled out of bed and stood on my feet. I pulled on a pair of workout shorts, put on a t-shirt, and slowly walked out of my bedroom headed for the kitchen. I grabbed the carafe from the coffee pot, filled it with water, and poured the contents into the top of the coffee pot. I reached up to the cabinet above the coffee pot and removed a filter and a can of Folgers coffee grounds. I opened the coffee basket, removed yesterday's filter filled with spent coffee grounds and threw it in the trash. I inserted a new filter, scooped coffee grounds into the basket, and switch on the coffee pot. While I waited for the carafe to fill with coffee, I walked over to the kitchen window and looked at my backyard.

Slivers of early morning sun illuminated parts of the lawn while others remained in dark shade. The trees were no longer ominous looking and stood peacefully, rising from the grass with dark trunks and interlaced branches extending mightily across the yard protecting the grass from the intense late–summer sun. Whatever had unnerved me last night was gone. I watched a brown squirrel race across the yard and quickly climb a tree trunk. While I felt hollow, the world seemed to be alive and moving on to a new day.

When I heard the coffee pot stop percolating, I turned around and walked over to the counter. I reached into the kitchen cabinet, grabbed a coffee mug, and poured a cup of steaming hot, black coffee. I walked out the back door and sat in one of the lawn chairs.

As I sipped my coffee, I could feel the warmth of the morning sunlight against my face. As the warmth against my cheeks soothed me, I recalled memories of my dad.

Wind was blowing through the open windows of my dad's gold 1970 Oldsmobile Cutlass as we drove down a narrow country road in Sagebrush. It was a bright sunny day with a clear blue sky. A field of sunflowers rushed by as I gazed out of the passenger window eating a strawberry Starburst, chewing it over and over. The radio played Seals and Croft's "Summer Breeze" which seemed to capture the moment in time as I savored the taste of strawberry in my mouth, mesmerized by big yellow and brown sunflowers corralled by barbed–wire fencing. "Summer breeze, makes me feel fine, blowin' through the jasmine in my mind."

I didn't have any idea where we were headed. My dad had a Schlitz beer tucked between his legs, and we just drove along country roads, many of which paralleled train tracks. He simply liked to get up on Saturdays and drive around looking for adventure with a cold beer tucked in his lap. I was happy. I loved car rides and definitely loved that strawberry Starburst.

I smiled to myself as I sipped my coffee. My dad was an eternal hippy, seeking a carefree life, free from rules, conformity, and restraints. If one lasting memory of him remained, it's how he freely floated outside of responsibility or consequences. He seemed to get away with things most of us would rot in jail for or die trying.

Chortling inwardly, I remembered a crazy night after we left a country house my dad's friend lived in. My dad recently finished rebuilding an old Dodge pickup, putting a hotrod motor into it in the process, and we had spent the afternoon showing it off.

When we left late at night, it was completely black outside the pickup. As I bounced up and down, jostled by bumps and turns along the road, all I could see was the glow of white lights from the dash. My dad had a can of beer in his lap and was playing "Let the Good Times Roll" by the Cars on the 8-track. On other occasions, I wasn't scared when he drove with a beer in his lap. On this night, I was terrified. It may have been my older age, but I sensed a wrongness and feared something bad would happen.

My dad drove recklessly, sliding sideways on corners and mashing the gas pedal when the road straightened. I had no idea how fast we were going, but the truck seemed to violently tremble as it floated over hills in the road. I couldn't see a thing except for dashboard lights against a black, moonless night.

As we approached the edge of Fort Myers, dim streetlamps illuminated a wide street. Songs from the Cars album played loudly while I sat silently feeling terrified, desperately wanting the carnival ride to end. We stopped at a red light. The glow of streetlights seemed bright and intense after being in the dark. When the light turned green, my dad stomped on the gas pedal, causing the pickup to accelerate quickly and squealing the tires in the process. As we approached what seemed like Mach 1 speed, blue and red lights began flashing behind us. My dad stiffened and yelled, "Oh shit!" while looking in the rearview mirror. Turning toward me, he said, "Hang on, we're not stopping—I'm not going to jail!"

We sped through town, running red lights. When my dad reached a highway ramp, he turned sharply, and the pickup seemed to lean sideways as we rounded a corner. He accelerated hard, and we seemed to walk away from the blue–and–red flashing lights. As we sped through the darkness, my dad frequently looked in his rearview mirror until he felt comfortable. After a while his body relaxed and he screamed "We did it, bud—ol' smokey couldn't keep up!"

Finishing my coffee, I wondered how many kids can say they rode with dear old Dad while he outran the cops. Raising my eyebrows, I wondered how many kids can say they watched *Smokey and the Bandit* from inside a semi-truck parked in the back of a drive-in movie theater.

Getting up from my chair, I walked into the house to take a shower and refresh myself before I called Jennifer to talk about arrangements and later went to see Sophia.

CHAPTER THREE

"Hello," a deep, tired voice answered.

"Hey, Vincent, it's James," I said. Vincent was Jennifer's husband. They'd been married for six years and had two little girls.

"How are you holding up, brother?" Vincent said with a sympathetic voice.

I sighed. "Oh, I've been better. I think right now I'm in shock, still trying to process all of it. It just seems surreal—you know?"

"Yeah, it's definitely weird. It's hard to believe he is gone. He called a couple days ago. He sounded kind of drunk but talked about the usual stuff. We just never thought—"

"How's Jennifer?"

"She's been in her bedroom all morning. She has bouts of crying. She called your mom earlier this morning and told her the news." Although my mom and dad had been divorced for some time, I knew the news would affect her. They were together for almost twenty years.

The thought of Mom left my shoulders feeling heavy. "Why did she call her so fast? I could have done that."

"Well, you know Jennifer. She just takes over and starts organizing everything."

Chortling, I replied, "Yes—I do know my sister. She probably has the funeral completely planned already." Shaking my head, I asked, "Is she able to talk?"

"I don't know. Let me go see."

The phone made a boom sound when it was set down on a hard surface. While I waited, I wondered how the kids were taking it. Riley was only five, and Sam was barely three. Likely they wouldn't understand. Our dad barely even saw Riley, and I didn't recall if he ever spent time with Sam. Seattle wasn't exactly close, so it was hard for all of us to get together. Good ol' alcohol. Generation one lives with it, and generation two misses out because of it.

"Hello," said Jennifer. Her voice sounded raspy and tired.

"Hey—how are you doing?"

"Better—I just can't stop crying."

"Yeah. I guess I'm not there yet. I think I'm too shocked to even feel anything. How did Mom take it?"

"Um—better than I expected. She didn't really say anything though. She just said to call if I needed anything."

"I'll give her some time to process and give her a call. Thankfully she has Jack around." My mom had been married to Jack for two years. He was a stability in her life that she really needed. After a brief pause, I continued, "So —do we need to do anything? I've never planned arrangements before. Is his body at the coroner's office? Do the police have any idea what happened?

"Actually, we don't need to do too much. The coroner has a link to a funeral home somewhere in Orlando. Once we decide on cremation or burial, they guide us through the arrangements and help find a plot. And no, they aren't telling me anything yet. They just said it is under investigation at this time and an autopsy will need to be performed. That's all they will say until they have more evidence of what actually happened."

"Really?" I said with an incredulous voice.

"Seriously, it shouldn't be too difficult."

"Wow—okay. Well, can I help with anything or call anyone?"

"Do you know how to get a hold of Tommy? The number I had for him is out of service."

I was not surprised she couldn't get a hold of Tommy! Our vagabond brother was about as elusive as an aardvark. "No—the last time I heard from Tommy he was in bad shape, drinking and strung out again." The thought of dealing with him vexed me. He was as bad as our dad.

"I will ask Mom. Anyone else?" I asked.

"Um—yes, I don't know how to get a hold of Uncle David or Aunt Patti."

"Hmm. Neither do I! I'll work on tracking them down this afternoon. I need to go see Sophia first."

Jennifer's voice brightened as she said, "Oh, yes! How are the plans coming along?"

"Okay. A Breckenridge wedding is expensive." Smiling, I continued, "We should have eloped and found a cheap Elvis in Las Vegas!"

"Oh, Jamie—you don't mean that. You two will be together a long time. Better to start your journey off with a beautiful wedding!" Jennifer was the only person who still called me Jamie.

"I don't mean that. I'm actually excited and looking forward to it. Sophia is my soul mate, and I can't imagine being with anyone else." Sighing heavily, I continued, "We had a fight yesterday because she wants kids, and well, you know how I feel about it. I don't want my kids to fall into the trap of addiction. I think there is real evidence that genetics plays a role in addiction."

"Jamie, you need to get over your crap! It's ridiculous. You are who you are, and just because Dad was an alcoholic and drug addict doesn't mean your kids will end up that way."

"Jennifer, I know—but look what happened to Tommy! He became just like Dad!"

"Yes—Tommy made a mess of his life. But again, that doesn't mean *your* children will end up addicts. They will have you as a good role model."

"What if I'm not as sane as you think?"

"No—you're nuts. But you are a good kind of nuts, and I love you. Sophia loves you, and your future kids will love you!"

Feeling flattered, I said, "Thank you! I'll go apologize to Sophia, and then tell her my dad is dead. Should be a fantastic conversation!"

She laughed. "Tell her hi for me."

"I will. Let me know if you hear anything from the coroner."

"Okay. Talk to you soon—Love you."

"Love you too!" I hung up the phone.

CHAPTER FOUR

When I got off the phone with my sister, I called Sophia and asked if I could come over and talk. She seemed surprised when I called. She didn't directly say it, but I think she expected me to be mad for a couple days.

I recombed my hair, brushed my teeth, and went out the back door, locking it before I stepped into the carport. The carport was another fine feature of the 1950s. Every time it snowed, I had to scoop snow drifts out before I could back the car out. I may as well have parked in the street when it snowed!

I briefly admired my blue Mustang with white racing stripes as I walked around to the driver's side door. I opened the door, slid into the bucket seat, and started the engine, which instantly roared to life, vibrating the whole car as the loud motor fast idled while warming up. The morning air was warm enough that the engine automatically adjusted to a quieter idle after thirty seconds.

After I backed out into the street, I put the car into drive and began my trek to Sophia's apartment. She is an eternal urbanite who lives in a seedy area near downtown Denver's Capitol Hill. Fearing for her safety and to no avail, I have implored her to move somewhere safer. Sophia is not only headstrong but simply loves to people watch. A delusional maniac walking down the street talking to himself is strangely delightful to her. I get it. Watching people behaviorally react and interact with each other is entertaining, and sometimes we find ourselves through studying the behavior of others. I just wished Sophia would peep the unawares in a safer place.

Traffic was light, and it didn't take long to arrive downtown. I found a tight spot along a nearby street and walked to Sophia's apartment building. It was a red brick building with a 1930s architectural design. It always makes me think of the haunted building in the 1980s movie *Ghostbusters*.

When I reached the inner doors of the apartment building, I pushed the buzzer for 402, and Sophia quickly buzzed me in. Rather than ride in the elevator, I walked the red carpeted stairs that spiraled upwards in a square shape. I don't trust elevators, and stairs keep me healthy.

As I walked down the hall, approaching Sophia's apartment, the door was open, and she was standing at the threshold waiting like she always did. And as always, I was enamored by her unique, ethnic looking beauty. She is short with long black curly hair, brown eyes, pouty red lips, and olive skin.

Sophia brightened with a smile as I approached. "Feeling better today?'

"Yes—you know I can never stay mad at you for long," I said. I reached my arms toward her and she quickly fell into my embrace. I held her tightly for a long moment and then moved her backwards while I planted a kiss on her lips. "I'm sorry about last night! Kids are something I wrestle with, but I'll work it out. I want to be with you, and if children will make you happy—then we will have children."

"James, you know I love you—I do. But I want *us* to have and raise children. . . together. I want you to be with me, not begrudgingly agreeing."

"Sophia, it's not that. I love children, but I am afraid I'll somehow screw them up. They are so trusting and fragile. What if. . . "

Sophia pressed her fingers to my lips. "Shh. . . I know you are afraid, but we will figure this out *together*. Maybe I don't know your brother, but I know you!" She stood up straight and put her hands on her hips. "And besides, I won't let you screw our kids up!"

Smiling, I said, "And that's why I love you!" I leaned forward and kissed her softly. "But there is so much you don't know about my family and if I told you *everything*, you would see why I don't want kids. . . "

Drawing back, grabbing my hand, and pulling me into the apartment, she said, "Come in—what did you want to talk to me about that couldn't be discussed over the phone?"

Remembering my dad's passing, I shifted my mood, becoming serious. Pushing the door closed, I said, "Honey, I think we should sit down for this."

Sophia's face darkened into a look of concern. "What is it? You're scaring me!"

As we both sat down on her plushy brown couch, I took her hands into mine and softly said, "My sister called last night and told me my dad was found dead in a motel room." As the words came out of my mouth, my eyes welled with tears.

"Oh, no," Sophia said, reaching to hug me. While her lips were close to my ear, she softly said, "I'm so sorry—are you okay?" I could feel the wetness of her tears against my cheek.

"I'm not sure—it feels so surreal. I've been thinking a lot about him since last night. I was so stressed over him coming back to Denver, and now I can't believe he's gone. And the thought of him dying horribly breaks my heart."

Withdrawing from her embrace, I told Sophia about my strange desire to listen to an old Billy Squier album and the sinister feeling I had in my backyard when I sensed a spirit standing in front of me. I shared some of the faded memories I recalled while I drank coffee this morning.

After I finished talking, Sophia said, "James, that's weird! You think it was really his spirit?"

Thinking of a ghost gave me goosebumps on the back of my neck. "Maybe. There was definitely something strange about all of it."

While her eyes looked to the side, she said, "I suppose it's possible. There are many things we don't know about the spiritual realm."

My eyes drifted upwards toward the ceiling while my thoughts turned inward. "Yes. . ."

"Well, I'm here for you, if you need to talk through things."

I wiped the moisture from my cheeks and sniffed my wet nose. "I know—I just need to process all of this and sort things out. Since last night I've been remembering a lot of stuff. And I don't even know when we can hold a funeral yet."

With an incredulous look, she said, "Why can't you have a funeral?"

"The coroner has to do an exam before they release the body. We don't really know any details yet."

"Goodness, James, that's strange!" Sophia stood up and

walked toward the kitchen. "I'm thirsty. Do you want anything to drink?"

Getting up to follow her, I said, "Yes. I'll have some water—my throat is dry."

Sophia and I talked a little more about my dad, and then we moved on to discussing the wedding plans in Breckenridge. We were supposed to get married in four months. As we got closer, time seemed to be moving faster.

The distraction felt cathartic for some reason.

CHAPTER FIVE

The next morning, I got up early and met Sophia for mass at St. Elizabeth's Cathedral. It is a beautiful church in the German Romanesque style. It was built in the 1870s by German immigrants who came to Denver looking for work in the railroad industry.

Following Sophia's prompting, I prayed about my dad's passing and asked the Lord to open my heart and help me overcome my fears. I asked for the Lord's grace as I sorted out my past, finding meaning in my dad's passing.

After church, Sophia and I spent the day walking around the 16th Street Mall window shopping. It was a hot day and heat radiated off the red bricks as we meandered through throngs of people. Sophia was energized by the activity. I just wanted to find some gelato and hide in a quiet corner. We compromised and found Ben and Jerry's Ice Cream and sat in metal chairs out on the sidewalk.

While eating my ice cream, I turned toward Sophia. "I'm not sure if I should go down to Orlando now or wait until the coroner's exam is completed," I said.

"I would wait. What if it takes a few weeks or something?"

"Yeah, I think you're right. I wonder how long it will take. . ." I stared upwards, noticing the tall downtown buildings, deep in thought.

CHAPTER SIX

I called my mom as soon as I got home from Sophia's on Sunday afternoon. She told me Tommy was in a rehab facility called Shady Pines. Even though I cringed at the thought of talking to him again, I called anyway.

"Good afternoon, Shady Pines," said a friendly sounding young man.

"Good afternoon. My name is James Fisher and I was told that my brother, Thomas Fisher is at your facility."

"Sir, we cannot give out any information regarding our patients."

I took in a deep breath to gather patience. "I understand that. But we have had a death in the family, and I need to speak with him. If I have called the correct facility, may I please speak with him?"

"Please hold." After a few minutes, the young man returned. "Sir, he is in a group therapy session right now. You can come to our facility tomorrow during visiting hours, which are between two and four p.m. Please be sure to have photo ID with you."

"Okay, I will come by tomorrow. Is the address 200 South Speer Boulevard?"

"Yes—we are one block down from Denver Cares."

"I know right where that is. I'll see you tomorrow. Thank you!" I'd picked up both dear ol' dad and Tommy from Denver Cares many times.

After I hung up the phone, I heated a cup of herbal tea in the microwave and walked outside to sit on the back porch. I wasn't even sure what I would say to Tommy. Something like this would likely send him over the edge.

CHAPTER SEVEN

I left work early and drove across town to Shady Pines. As I pulled into the parking lot, I could see a single–level, U–shaped building with a low–pitched roof. The facility was surrounded by green grass, shrubs, and large maple trees. The open area behind the facility was secured by tall, wrought–iron fencing.

When I entered the doors, I had to stop before a second set of doors and push a buzzer for assistance.

"Can I help you?" a woman asked in a serious tone.

"Yes, I am here to see Thomas Fisher." After a brief pause, the door buzzed and I opened it. As I walked through the door, I saw a small lobby and reception desk to the right.

"Sir, please fill out this check–in form. Do you have photo ID?" asked a short, fortyish woman with black hair.

I reached into my back pocket and grabbed my wallet. "Yes, I have it right here." After a couple of tugs, my driver's license slid out, and I handed it to her.

"Thank you." The woman walked over to a photo copier

and made a copy of my license while I completed the sign–in form. When she came back and saw that I was finished, she said, "Please take a seat. A staff member will come and get you. We require visitors to be escorted while on premises." Her statement seemed reasonable. Patients probably try to have friends sneak in dope all the time.

I walked over to a chair and sat down.

After a few minutes, a young man who looked like he was in his mid-twenties came through a door opposite from the reception desk. "Sir—if you will follow me."

"Sure." I got up and walked toward the young man.

As I approached, the young man extended a hand toward me and said, "My name is Scott. I will take you to the visiting lounge."

I shook Scott's hand. "Nice to meet you. I am James Fisher." As Scott turned, I followed him through the door and down a long corridor with a white, clinical looking floor. I noticed patient rooms with open doors as we walked. It was as quiet as a mausoleum.

When we approached a large lounge room at the end of the hall, Scott gestured for me to enter and said, "Thomas will be in shortly."

The lounge area had the same white flooring. There were a few round tables with white plastic chairs around them. Couches with orange cushions lined a couple of the walls. There was a TV mounted in one of the corners displaying a talk show, and some of the patients were shooting pool and playing foosball in the back of the room. Thinking Tommy and I would need some privacy, I walked over to a couch that was the farthest away from other people.

A few minutes had passed; Tommy walked in wearing a pair of loose-fitting jeans and a dark blue t-shirt. He had a full beard, and his brown hair had grown long, looking shaggy and chaotic. As he approached, I noticed he had bags under his hazel eyes, and lines were forming on his face. He looked older than me. I stood to greet him.

"What are you doing here?" Tommy asked with aggressive, wild, staring eyes.

"Nice to see you too, brother! I need to talk to you."

"I don't want to hear anything Mom's perfect, golden child has to say!"

I breathed in deeply. As much as I wanted to throw him through a wall, I knew this wasn't the time to get into an argument with him. "Tommy, I'm not here to argue with you. I need to talk to you about something." I gestured to the couch. "Can we sit down for a minute?"

Tommy hesitated for a moment and then quickly walked to the couch. "Make it quick!"

We sat on opposite ends of the couch. I paused while I tried to find the right words. "Tommy, there really isn't an easy way to say this—so I'm just going to say it. Dad passed away." As I uttered the words, Tommy's hands began to shake, and his bottom lip quivered. A tear slid down his right cheek.

"What happened?" Tommy asked in a shaky voice.

Seeing Tommy's distress, I replied in a thoughtful-sounding voice, "Tommy, we don't know all the details yet, but we were told he was found in a motel room."

"Oh. . ." Tommy brought a hand up to his mouth, and he began to sob, his shoulders shaking. "Who—who would do something like that?"

I slid closer to him. "We don't know. My guess is that it was random. Listen—I don't want you to worry about all this right now. Just focus on getting yourself cleaned up."

Tommy sniffed his nose. "Don't worry about me Jamie —I don't need your pity! When is the funeral?"

"We don't know yet."

"What do you mean you *don't* know?"

"They are still investigating and holding his body. We can't figure anything out until that's done. Jennifer and I can fly you down after the arrangements are made."

"I'll pay you back. I don't want to be owing you anything."

"Tommy—don't worry about it. We're family. . ."

He abruptly stood up. "I need to get to group. Thanks for coming by and letting me know." Before I could stand up to hug him, he turned and walked toward the door.

I got up and slowly walked over to the door and asked a staff member nearby to escort me out. My heart felt heavy with the realization that Tommy was still angry with me. He always blamed everyone else for his screw-ups. It wasn't my fault he chose to use cocaine while I was letting him sleep on my couch. I told him he could stay with me until he got himself back on his feet, but he had to stay clean. He didn't stay clean, and I had to throw him out. He never even realized how hard that was for me!

CHAPTER EIGHT

Toward the end of the week, Jennifer called me and said the coroner's exam was complete, and they would release his body while they finalized the report. She was now working with a funeral home to make arrangements. However, they told her we couldn't cremate the body until the coroner's report was released and the police completed their investigation. A police detective named Allen Daniels had apparently called Jennifer and asked strange questions about our dad. It sounded like we wouldn't get any information until we arrived in Orlando.

While on the call, I briefed Jennifer on my latest developments. I tracked down Uncle David and Aunt Patti and shared the news. They said they would make travel arrangements once we knew more. Uncle David was living in Galveston, Texas, and Aunt Patti was living in Ann Arbor, Michigan. As my dad was the outcast of the family, we barely knew them. I also told her about my visit with Tommy. She agreed that we would fly him down to Orlando once arrangements were made. Jennifer thought it might be a good idea to have him fly down with Mom and Jack.

After I ended the phone call with Jennifer, I called Sophia and then my boss. I told Sophia I wanted to drive down to Orlando and have some downtime before I dealt with everything. She thought that was a good idea and encouraged me to take some time to myself. When the arrangements were made, she would fly down to meet me.

The discussion with my boss was far more intense than I expected. After he extended a half–hearted, clumsy condolence, he asked who would back me up while I was out for two weeks. I conveyed to him that as always, the other guys could handle issues when I wasn't around. I was happy to end the call and looked forward to a long quiet three–day drive to Orlando.

CHAPTER NINE

As I sat in the Mustang letting it warm up, I quickly ran through a mental checklist ensuring I hadn't forgotten anything. I mentally checked my luggage, whether or not I locked up the house, turned off the coffee pot, left the sprinkler system on, double checked all faucets ensuring they were off, asked Clyde my next door neighbor to keep an eye on things, put a bag of change in the glove box for the tolls in Kansas. . .

Once I was satisfied that I had everything and was ready to go, I anxiously backed the Mustang out of the driveway, hoping I hadn't forgotten anything. I drove to the gas station, topped off the gas tank, and meandered through side streets to the highway onramp. I faced nine hours of Colorado and Kansas. I planned to stay overnight in Kansas City and then get up the next morning and drive to Atlanta, Georgia, where I'd stay in a motel. The drive from Atlanta to Orlando was only six hours, which gave me enough time to locate a good hotel to stay in for the week.

The sky overhead was covered in blueish–gray clouds,

and rain periodically fell. Colorado needed the moisture, as the blazing summer heat turned once–beautiful green grass into withered remnants of life. The grayness of the day created an inner fog within me. It was the sort of day where I wanted to crawl under the covers and sleep. Instead, I drank coffee from my thermos, attempting to repress early morning fatigue.

The drive out of the city's labyrinth was uneventful as the only traffic around me were early–morning bread trucks, Royal Crest milk deliveries, Walmart semis, and construction workers scurrying to job sites. Once I passed Strasburg and Byers, Colorado's landscape became monotonous with flat grassy pastures dotted with trees and bushes. Interesting sites were the occasional cylinder–shaped granaries, surrounded by farmland, electricity–producing wind turbines, and the steady caravan of semi-trucks. The monotony gave me ample time to think.

Sophia didn't know everything. She didn't know about the crazy stories that filled my childhood or my struggles while in college.

Addiction is the all–consuming beast within, and the accompanying flames will immolate the daring trespasser who encounters its deceptive path. Addiction never happens all at once in one moment. No—it's a slow process. First you are deceptively lured to the tunnel entrance, enticed by curiosity and thrill–seeking pleasure, and as you wander deeper, the darkness becomes so enveloping that you can't see your way out. You're trapped. That was why I was afraid of its seed passing to my offspring, and why Sophia's desire for children scared me.

Shortly after high school graduation, my own deceptive journey began when my first love abruptly snuffed out our flame and moved on to other adventures. The internal change didn't happen overnight. It was a gradual process as I met new friends in college and attended wild parties.

During my first year in college, the parties were innocuous. Mostly it was small groups, drinking Busch light, dragging cigarettes, and taking occasional swigs from a passed liquor bottle while people intermingled, engaged in small talk, or animatedly debated profound topics. Usually topics centered around conspiracy theories with randomly linked events. A few parties later, someone added the fun game of smoking pot and partaking in the zipper ride. This was a game where you first smoked some pot and then stood upright with your eyes closed and your arms stretched outwards. Then a strange dizzy feeling would rush upon you and it would feel like you were riding on a common amusement park ride called the Zipper. It was a simple, giggly thrill.

During my second year in college, parties became less about achieving a light buzz and conversing, and more about getting screwed up. We played drinking games, pounding beer after beer. We smoked mounds of pot and dabbled in hallucinogens. As parties grew, newcomers came. Often, they arrived with cocaine or methamphetamine. I wandered deeper into the circle, and the rooms became darker, often illuminated by black lights. As the rooms became darker, mornings arrived later, and I became more tired, too tired to study or get homework done. When I complained to my new circle of friends that I struggled to keep up with homework, exams, and final essays, they gathered around and supported me as good friends do, offering me speed and cocaine to stay alert. For a while, I functioned with the help of my friends and wandered deeper into the cave. Of course, as I took more speed to wake up from last night's party, I needed to drink alcohol or smoke pot to come down from amphetamines when the homework was completed. The cycle was endless and miserable.

Two months into my third year of college, I was burned out and felt miserable. The more I partied, the crappier I felt. The so–called friends I met during my first year of college had moved on, and I had acquired an improved circle of idiot friends. Oh, these friends were great. They shared in your misery and even picked the color of your casket out. At least that is how I felt at the time. I felt like the walking dead and one day I abruptly decided to quit playing with my friends.

The journey out of the cave was slow. I was surrounded by utter darkness with no sense of direction. Propelled by a deep desire to get out, I stumbled along, confused and alone. My internal locus of control at the time was some-thing automatic. It was as if my life switched to autopilot. Eventually, I found the light at the entrance and walked out. But the light was different, and the landscape changed.

I met Sophia around the time I was emerging from the cave. I still wore long, shaggy hair and dressed like a Seattle grunge musician. Both of us were working for an informa-tion technology company as co-ops performing mundane work. Sophia was frequently tasked with filing, and I was often tasked with courier duties or switching out 9–track tapes on a Honeywell DPS system older than I was. Sophia attended Denver University, majoring in mathematics with a minor in computer science, and I was attending the University of Colorado at Denver, majoring in computer information systems, with a minor in business.

The night I met Sophia we were both enjoying two–dollar margaritas and all–you–can–munch–on chips and salsa with co-workers during happy hour at a bar on the roof of a Mexican restaurant. With her ethnic beauty and sultry voice, I was mesmerized. I wanted to go talk to her but wrestled with what to say. I vividly recalled the guy named Daryl telling me I didn't have a chance in hell at getting her number. Well, I couldn't let a dare go unchecked, so I sauntered over to her table and performed my best flirting. Poor Daryl didn't know how far I would go to win a bet.

"Hi," I said.

With a confused look on her face, Sophia said, "Um—hi. And you are?"

"James."

"It is nice to meet you, James. What brings you to our table?"

"You." I flashed a playful smile.

"Oh, really?"

With a chuckle, I said, "Yes. I couldn't take my eyes off of you and just had to talk to you."

"Is that the best you got? Perhaps my name is Candy. . ."

I laughed. "Well, the truth is, I have had a crush on you for a while," I said sheepishly. I nodded in the direction of Daryl. "Do you see that guy sitting over there wearing a blue Polo?"

Craning her neck, Sophia said, "Yes."

"Well, he bet me twenty bucks I couldn't get your number." Sophia looked at me with a smirk but remained quiet for a moment.

"And you like to win bets. . ."

"I do!" I stood up straight, feigning confidence. "Look, I'll split it with you. Just scribble a bogus number on the napkin —he'll never know. Or. . ." I shrugged and leaned closer. "You could give me your real number, and I could win and call you."

Sophia pursed her lips with a smirk and arched eyebrows. She seemed entertained and incredulous at the same time. "You're a dork, you know that, right?"

I nodded with a smile in silence.

"Okay, I'll give you my number. But—instead of giving me half, you can buy me dinner."

Sophia and I had dinner in the Mexican restaurant later that evening, laughing and getting to know one another. We went out a few times after that, but then we kind of drifted apart without dating. Five years would pass before I seriously dated her, which in hindsight was for the best as I had a little bit more stumbling to do on the path of life.

Over a period of six months, I eluded the old circle of friends until they faded away, moving on to other recruits. Slowly, I internally healed myself and rediscovered the light of day. My mother had dedicatedly taken me to church every Sunday when I was growing up, but I had turned away from God and what I viewed as self-righteous, holy roller ideals. What I didn't realize at the time was that turning from God only propelled me deeper into the world's lies and deceptions. And when the time came to navigate extreme darkness, I lacked a moral compass or a lighted path. It was within the struggle that I came to understand the importance of faith and spirituality. Unfortunately, that understanding would arrive much later, around the time Sophia and I found each other again.

Once I picked up the shattered pieces of my life and learned how to navigate life sober again, I brought my grades up and graduated with a low B average. I began putting in extra hours with my employer and moved up to a desktop technician position, answering technical calls and repairing computers. The decent pay afforded me a nicer apartment in a pleasant foothills neighborhood on the outskirts of Denver. I began working out like I did in high school, lifting weights and hiking the woodsy trails near my apartment.

The irony of my own struggles was that they arrived after many years of judging my dad's struggles and failures. While praying alongside Sophia, I often asked if I was being shown understanding. God never let me wander too far away, and looking back, I realized that Jesus was alongside me at every step. It was as if I was being allowed to stumble for a greater purpose and then awaked by a thunderous voice within my head saying, "DO YOU UNDERSTAND?" What I understood was that addiction seemed to pass from generation to generation like a virulent disease. After all I had seen and lived through growing up, how could I fall prey to addiction when I knew it so well?

After driving eastward for a couple of hours, I could no longer suppress the urge to pee and quickly exited the highway to a gas station on the edge of Goodland, Kansas. Semi-trucks paralleled each other on the back side. Likely the truck drivers were patrons of the attached diner.

CHAPTER TEN

After I relieved myself, I filled the car up with gas and purchased a couple strips of countertop beef jerky and headed up the onramp to the highway.

The blueish–gray sky had transformed into a hazy but sunny day. A giant rainbow stretched across the sky with ends on sundried, grassy Kansas pastureland. I remained deep in thought, wandering through gardens of the past.

My brother Tommy was our dad's clone. Throughout high school, he was constantly in trouble. During his freshman year, he was frequently caught ditching and smoking cigarettes and flunked a few of his classes. Even though Mom made him go to summer school, he marched into his sophomore year with the same attitude, except that year he began smoking pot behind the school with the skater kids. Mom thought a job would help teach him some responsibility, so she helped him get a job as a bagger at the grocery store near our house. Of course, he screwed that up when he got caught smoking pot with his friends behind the store. During his junior year, he ditched nearly a month of school. In fact, his ditching became so flagrant that mom escorted him to school a few mornings in the hopes public embarrassment would make him fearful of ditching. To our mom's disappointment, it didn't. He kept ditching and later that year was thrown out of school and ticketed for smoking pot at school. Tommy's senior year was the same. He barely graduated, only because the teachers were sick of dealing with him and let him slide.

I remembered an argument he had with our mom one morning:

"Tommy—get your butt out of bed! You have school today and I need to drop you off earlier so I can get to work," Mom yelled from the middle of the stairs.

Tommy stomped out his bedroom wearing nothing but sweat pant bottoms that barely hung on his hips. His hair was a frizzed–out mess and he looked like a deranged homeless person. "I told you I don't want to go!" Tommy screamed.

"And I said you are going anyway! You're not dropping out of school!"

"I don't want to go to school anymore! School is boring, and my teachers are morons. I hate school!"

"You need to finish school. You want to work low paying labor jobs the rest of your life? Seems like all you want to do anymore is sit around smoking pot. Well, that's not going to happen in this house! Maybe we need to get you into drug counseling. You are starting out just like your father did, and look where that led."

"I won't be like Dad! I'm not going to be an addict. I know how to control things and use a little bit at a time!"

"Well, son, that's what all addicts say and believe when they start out. It's not going to happen to me. Your dad said the

same thing. The next thing you know you can't stop, and you will want to experiment with much harder drugs."

"NO, I won't—smoking a little pot once in a while helps me deal with life. I get stressed out at school. It helps me relax, and it's fun to get high."

"Tommy, you need to learn how to cope with stress in life and find productive ways to relieve stress. You will always have stress in life, and it's best if you learn how to cope with it now!"

"See, that's what I mean. You are always preaching at me and won't just let me do my own thing. I'm not like Jamie or Jennifer! I wish you'd see that for once!"

"Honey—I see that you struggle with things, and that's why I want to help you," Mom said.

"Just leave me alone! I hate school, and I hate being here!"

Mom looked at her watch. "I don't have time for this! I have an important meeting at work this morning. Get in the shower, and be ready to go in twenty minutes! You will go to school and follow rules while you are in this house!"

In a huff, Tommy stalked into the bathroom and slammed the door.

"Don't slam the door," Mom yelled.

After Tommy graduated, he floundered for a year getting high and sleeping half the day. When our mom had finally had enough, she kicked him out of the house. Since then, he's overstayed his welcome with friends, lived on the streets, spent time in jail, and floated in and out of rehab. Tommy followed in Dad's footsteps.

Jennifer and I remained close throughout our childhood. Even though we lived almost two states apart as adults, we remained close, often calling to check up on each other. As our childhood and teenage years were chaotic and ever changing, we supported each other when there wasn't anyone else to depend on. Mom was like a sturdy anchor that kept the ship in place while the seas raged, but our dad also overwhelmed her with his insanity, often requiring all of her focus and attention.

My relationship with Tommy became tumultuous during his teenage years. Even though he is four years younger than I am, we played together as kids. We rode bikes around the neighborhood, climbed trees in our backyard, played board games, and went sledding together in the wintertime.

When Tommy entered seventh grade, he began to change, choosing to hang out with problem kids who ditched school and smoked. He seemed to embrace the rebellious life while I avoided it. The more he upset Mom, the meaner I became toward him. Sometimes I would hold him down and poke at his chest violently with my finger. Other times, I shoved him to the ground and repeated shoving him down each time he tried to get up. Dad was enough; we didn't need his crap too. Maybe I was too mean, but he offered nothing but chaos when I wanted stability.

Later when he was in high school, I matured and had a change of heart. I tried to help him change, suggesting sports and weight lifting with me. But he wouldn't have anything to do with me by then. He'd found his dope–fiend friends, and they became his family.

I didn't blame him for his anger, but no matter how hard I tried, I couldn't fix it. The deeper he sank into addiction, the more he hated me for being an achiever. He called me so many names. . . douchebag, sporto, materialistic, uptight. . . the list went on. I couldn't blame him though. He simply inherited Dad's addiction genes and couldn't help himself. The monkey was on his back from the beginning.

As I drove along I-70 approaching Kansas City, the highway began to widen into more lanes, and traffic became heavier. On the distant horizon, I could see the tall cylindrical buildings in downtown Kansas City. I was hungry and tired, and the Mustang was nearing an empty gas tank, so I exited the highway to a gas station, knowing I might need to drive around for a while searching for a fast food joint and cheap motel near the highway.

After I replenished the Mustang's gas tank, I drove down the street until I found a Burger King. As I entered the drive-thru I rolled down my window and immediately recognized the familiar smell of charred burger mixed with smoke. The smell made my stomach rumble, and I suddenly felt famished. Sitting in a car for nine hours is hard work. When my turn arrived, I ordered a large Whopper meal intending to eat it once I found a motel. What actually happened was that I parked in the lot and devoured my food. My willpower was shot, and I was incredibly hungry.

Sipping my large Coke, I drove out of the parking lot in an after–meal daze and feeling sleepy. I couldn't find a motel on the street Burger King was on, so I drove back to the highway and headed deeper into the city. About three exits later, I located a motel called the Economy Lodge, advertising free internet and a continental breakfast. Free always enticed me, so I pulled in.

The business office was a beige, rectangular, smooth stucco building with a tall canopy in front of the doors. Near the office was a small square patch of lush, green grass with a red–bricked flower garden. The business office was encircled by separate rectangular buildings with two levels of brown–doored rooms facing the parking lot.

When I checked in, I was given a key to 402C. I smiled when they gave me the key, as it was a peculiar number and very familiar, as Sophia's apartment number was 402. Slack with fatigue, I drove the car to my assigned lodge and hefted my luggage to the room.

CHAPTER ELEVEN

Refreshed from a long, hot, steamy shower, I dressed in a pair of shorts and a t-shirt. I was missing Sophia and longed to hear her voice.

The room smelled like stale cigarettes mixed with the typical mustiness found in old buildings. Cities were just beginning to ban smoking in public places, and judging by the smell of the room, it would take years for lingering smell of cigarettes to fade. Society may have to tear down buildings and rebuild to eliminate the smell of cigarettes. It's amazing how smoke binds and imbues itself to everything it wafts into.

Sitting on the bed, I picked up my cell phone from the brown end table and dialed Sophia's number. I chuckled when I saw the commonly placed bible lying on the end table near the lamp stand. When I think of hotel rooms, I think of seedy places where adultery–committing couples secretly entangle their sordid passions. I rarely think of someone stopping for the night, becoming overtly religious, and reading the bible.

"Hello." Sophia's voice soothed me.

"Hey," I said, raising the pitch of my voice.

"I was hoping you would call! I have been praying you drove safely today."

"I made it. I'm at a motel in Kansas City. It was a long drive without much to see," I said in a tired voice. "How was your day?"

"Busy at work. One of my colleagues needed help figuring out why an array in their program was not outputting the correct values. After adding breakpoints throughout the code and digging for hours, we found an error in an equation which was producing incorrect values."

Chuckling, I said, "That is exactly why I never wanted to be a programmer. A tedious problem like that would have driven me bananas! No, thanks. I'll stick to the systems side."

"Programming is fun! It's like solving a puzzle each day."

"I'll take your word for it. I don't have the brain for it. But you—you like numbers, and I can see why you would find programming entertaining."

"Enough about me. Work is work. I want to hear about you. Did you have time to think about things?"

I thought the question odd. All I had was time to think on my highway sabbatical. "Yes, I thought a lot about my college years and stuff. Do you remember the first night I met you in Jose's?"

"Yes—you were cocky and had some silly line about betting your friend. I would have ignored your flirts if you hadn't seemed endearing."

Shrugging my shoulders, I said, "I'm always sweet!"

"Sometimes you are sweet. Other times you are a pain in the. . . "

"Hey!"

Chortling, Sophia said, "But I love you anyway! And by the way, you didn't need a line that night. I noticed you when you walked in with your friend."

Stunned by that revelation, I asked, "You did?"

Sophia chuckled and said, "Yes! You were such a dork and oblivious. I liked you before that even. You just never noticed."

I thought about my college partying years. I was so caught up with my own world that I didn't even notice anyone around me. In a surprised voice, I said, "Wow—I had no idea."

"Well, it doesn't matter—we are together now!" After a brief pause, she continued in a more serious tone, "James, while praying for you today I remembered a passage from the book of 1 Peter I once read. It said, 'They stumble by disobeying the word, as is their destiny.' The Old Testament was filled with stories conveying the idea that we are given spiritual destinies chosen by God before we are born. There was a sense of predestination within them. But in Peter's letter, he pointed out that while the disobedient behave just as predicted, those who freely choose to change—can. You don't have to be what was predetermined."

Sophia's words spurred thoughts of my life and what I saw while growing up. Somehow, she always knew what to say and when to say it. "Hmm—that's an interesting idea."

In a serious tone, Sophia said, "James, just think about it. You are much too fearful over things you can't control. God gave you free choice, not the ability to control everything around you."

I laughed. "It sure would be nice though!"

"Will you just think about this?"

"Yes, I will. Thank you."

"Okay," she said in a satisfied voice. "What time do you leave tomorrow?"

"I hope to get out of here by seven. I never sleep well in strange places, so we'll see."

"Well, try and sleep tonight and drive safely. Will you call me tomorrow and let me know you are safe?"

"Yes. I wish you were with me. I hate being this far away from you!"

"Me too. I'll see you in two days though."

"Not soon enough."

"Okay, we'll talk tomorrow. I love you!"

"I love you more! Blowing a kiss your way," I said, gesturing a blown kiss alone in my motel room.

"Goodnight!"

"Goodnight," I said and switched my cell phone off.

Allowing Sophia's voice to linger in my mind, I looked around the motel room, noticing the tacky brown curtains, the carpet with alternating shades of brown rectangles, and the dark brown bureau with a TV on top.

Grabbing a couple more of the pillows and shoving them behind me, I decided to call Jennifer. Sophia's comment only stirred up more thoughts within me, and I wanted to work some of them out with her.

While my new cell phone plan limited me to 450 daytime minutes each month, I now had unlimited talk minutes at night. I may as well use them.

I dialed my sister's number and waited while the phone rang.

"Hello," Jennifer said.

"Hey, it's me!" I replied.

Her voice brightened as she said, "Hi, Jamie! How is the drive going?"

"Okay, I guess. Today it was just one long stretch of flat, grassy pastures from Denver to Kansas City. Not much to look at," I said, laughing.

Sighing, she said, "Ugh—I don't like long drives. I'd rather just pay extra and fly."

"It wasn't about money. I just wanted some time to myself and think."

"And did you get some good thinking in today?"

"Yes—lots of it!" Pausing briefly, I continued with a hesitant voice. "Hey—can we talk about Dad? I have been thinking about what I should say in the eulogy, and the more I thought about it, the more I began to remember all of the crap that happened."

"Um—sure. What did you want to talk about?"

"Well—do you remember all of the stuff that happened over the years?"

"Some—bits and pieces. I tried to block a lot of it out."

"I would love that ability. Unfortunately, I soaked the memories up like a sponge and remember everything! I just remember how everything kept getting worse and worse. I remember being little and riding in the back of an old Dodge with Tommy while Dad and Uncle John drove around in the country on a hot summer day drinking beer and stuff. When we got home, Mom asked us what we did, and Tommy and I told her we just drove around while Uncle John and Dad drank beer. When Mom yelled at Dad, he got mad and told us he'd never take us anywhere." I began to chuckle. "Can you imagine yelling at a couple of little kids that snitched you out for drinking and driving? You'd think that would be your wakeup call!"

"It would for me!"

"Right! But then things got worse. I remembered waking up one morning and Dad's pickup that he spent months fixing up was sitting on a trailer in the driveway all smashed and destroyed. I distinctly remember seeing an empty bottle of peppermint schnapps laying in the driveway. When dad got out of bed, he was all banged up and hunched over with a limp. He never said, but I remember hearing someone say he was thrown out of the truck and it rolled over him."

"I don't remember any of that. I think I was too little."

"Yeah—I doubt you'd remember a lot about that."

"Um—the earliest memory I have is when Mom got pissed at Dad when his friends came over on Christmas Eve to party. She was so upset that she took us to stay at Aunt Maggie's that night." After a pause, Jennifer joked, "Santa didn't come that Christmas!"

"I remember that. It was a gray sunless day, and it felt the same way in the house. It was like Dad was stumbling around in the dark and didn't see us! Do you remember being dragged out of the house in the middle of the night and going with Mom to the police station to bail him out of jail?"

"Um—vaguely. I remembered the times Mom kicked him out, and he stayed with weird druggy friends. I always hated visiting him."

"Oh—yeah, I do remember that. One weekend he told Mom he wanted to spend time with us, and when we went over to the guy's townhouse, Dad disappeared and left us alone all weekend. That's another thing I remember—disappearing for days and days."

"Yeah, Dad was crazy. But what's the point of rehashing all this?"

"What do I say in a eulogy? Thanks, Dad, for all the wonderful memories and happy–ass circus life!"

"Jamie, it wasn't all bad. He took us to movies, and he took you to drag races and car shows sometimes."

Feeling a heaviness within my heart, I sighed. "I know. I don't think of him as a monster or hate him. I think my issue is that I saw the escalation and how he was consumed by addiction. No matter how many warning signs flashed, he couldn't stop it, and we had to live through his decisions. It just scares me to think I might screw up my own kids with stuff like that."

"Jamie, you are not Dad. Just because he was an addict doesn't mean you will be one. You have done a lot with your life and made good choices."

"Sometimes!" I thought about my own rebellion and struggles during college.

"Take what you learned and teach your kids the right way to live. It will all turn out okay!"

"Maybe you're right. I certainly never wanted to become like that. Do you think there is a gene or something that gets passed down? Think about it. Our grandparents were alcoholics and we have aunts and uncles who became alcoholics. I wonder if Dad inherited the *addiction gene*."

"Maybe. But I think we all have choices. We can choose to not fall into those things."

"I suppose." I resigned myself to that thought. "So, what are you doing tonight?"

"Well, after I get the kids to bed, I plan to read a book I just bought."

"Sounds relaxing. Have you heard from the coroner at all?"

"No. I think they were mad this morning when I called again. I'll just wait until they finalize the report."

"I'm curious to know what happened."

"Me too. Something is weird in this."

"Definitely. Well, I'm gonna let you go. I need to get some sleep tonight. I have a long drive to Atlanta tomorrow."

"Well, drive safe! And Jamie—let this stuff go! It doesn't matter. He had his life, and you have yours."

"I know. Thanks, sis! I'll talk to you soon."

"Okay, goodnight!" The phone clicked dead, and my cell phone ended the call.

I felt drained of energy. I got up, brushed my teeth, and went to bed.

CHAPTER TWELVE

When I awoke the next morning, I was groggy. I tossed and turned all night, floating in and out of sleep. My neck and back were sore from the squishy, unsupportive bed that dipped in the middle. The pillows were horrible. I tried four of them with the same uncomfortable result. Each time my head would sink to the bed with the sides of the pillow rising up against the sides of my head. Who can sleep like that?

Throwing the covers off of me, I rolled out of bed and stiffly walked around the room looking for a coffee pot. I found a one-cup in the bathroom that had two instant coffee packets. I filled up the pot and brewed one of them.

I switched on the TV and flipped channels until I discovered a *Friends* re-run. Chuckling while Ross screamed, "We were on a break," I sipped my hot coffee, not thinking —just laughing.

When I finished my cup of coffee, I showered, collected my belongings, and hefted the luggage down to the Mustang. I walked over to the main office, checked out and then ate a wimpy continental breakfast that featured muffins, little boxes of cereal and slightly cold milk, and bananas.

Annoyed with my less than satisfactory breakfast, I filled a medium sized–cup with black coffee that was thick as tar and smelled burnt, and headed back to the highway. I faced an eleven–hour drive.

CHAPTER THIRTEEN

The sky was clear blue and sunny. I enjoyed the sights throughout the morning and early afternoon. I saw the Budweiser factory and the Gateway Arch while I drove through St. Louis and delighted in the green grasses and dark green–leaved trees in Nashville. Everything seemed new and entertaining to my eyes. I didn't really think about my dad, Sophia, my family, or anything else. The panoramic distractions alongside the road distracted me until I heard Bob Seger's song "Sunburst" play on the radio. As soon as I heard the dark melodies and Bob Seger's raspy voice, I was transported back in time and remembered coming home from school one day.

Jennifer, Tommy, and I walked home from school like usual. Fall had arrived and intermittent gusts of wind blew the leaves around. As the three of us ambled up the street toward our house, grayish–white clouds blanketed the sky, obscuring the sunlight. The weird lighting made things around us look ordinary. Even the green lawns and colorful leaves appeared bland.

When we arrived home, I retrieved the key to our back door hidden under a rock in the backyard. As I unlocked the door to let Jennifer and Tommy into the house, I noticed a weird sign on the garage door that read, Do not disturb, testing in progress. Even though the sign seemed ominous, making me suspicious and sense something was wrong, I followed Jennifer and Tommy into the house. As they rumbled around the house throwing bags, grabbing snacks, and turning on the TV, I stood in the back room, fretting over whether or not to go out to the garage. After a few minutes, I followed my instincts and walked out of the house toward the garage door.

As I neared it, I heard a low hum that sounded like an engine idling. I was in seventh grade and knew that a car running in the garage was not safe—or normal. I knocked on the door and heard my dad say, "Stay out. I'm working." I didn't say anything in return. I quietly turned and walked back into the house trying to process the strange situation.

I puttered around the house for fifteen minutes or so but couldn't shake the ominous feeling I had. Something was wrong, but I didn't know what it was. Deciding I needed to investigate the garage, I walked back to the garage door and knocked. There was no answer. Sensing something bad, I opened the garage door and was immediately over-whelmed by the noxious smell of exhaust fumes. The whole garage was filled with smoke flowing from the exhaust pipes. I ran into the garage, fanning smoke away from my face with my right hand. Bob Seger was playing on the stereo in the garage as I glimpsed my dad's legs under the truck. Immediately an alarm bell sounded in my head, and I quickly raced to open the big garage door and get the smoke out. I frantically grabbed my dad by his ankles and leaned back while I dragged his heavy body out from under the truck. When I got him out from under the truck, I realized he was unconscious. I didn't know what to do, so I grabbed his wrists and dragged him out the big door and through the yard gate with all my might. I was nearly out of breath as I put my ear to his mouth to see if he was breathing. He was, but I had no idea what to do next. I didn't know CPR or anything.

I left my dad lying in the backyard and ran into the house screaming, "Jennifer, Jennifer, call an ambulance! Hurry!"

As Jennifer walked out of the front living room into the kitchen, she said, "What happened—what for?"

"Just do it! Dad is unconscious, and I don't have any idea what to do!"

Jennifer's eyes widened big as she looked at me. She quickly picked up the phone and dialed 911. When they answered, I faintly heard her say, "My dad is unconscious, and we need help!" as I ran back out to the yard.

When I reached my dad, he was still lying on the grass, not moving, barely breathing.

It seemed like an eternity passed before the paramedics arrived. Just as they were loading him into the ambulance, my mom pulled up. While I was in the backyard, Jennifer had called her at work and told her what was going on.

Dad spent several days in the hospital in a barometric chamber because of carbon monoxide poisoning. When he was finally released from the hospital, he started attending AA meetings and went to counseling for a short while. But then the drinking started back up, and he eventually drove the suicide pickup off a deserted highway and flipped it. The response was the same as all the other wrecks. He somehow walked away from the accident just sore and bruised. The car or truck was a piece of crap and he could have been killed. I don't think he ever admitted to himself that his drunk driving was at fault and not the vehicle. There was always something or someone to blame.

The following year, he left for Arizona in an attempt to escape the mess he'd made for himself. He thought if he started fresh in a new environment and got away from his drinking buddies, things would be different. He wasn't aware of that old saying, "Wherever you go, there you are."

The fact was, my dad was a dysfunctional alcoholic and drug user. His life was a whirlwind that often left his family to pick up the pieces. But that's what substance abuse does! It puts a bubble around the addict, and everyone around them plays a part—revolving around them and constantly picking up the pieces. When I was growing up, I had to be on guard, waiting for the next crisis, the lies, the constant deceptions, the emotional rollercoaster rides, the fear, the disappointment, and the avoidance of my own needs and feelings because I was too busy coddling his.

I never wanted that for my kids. Was that so wrong? Why couldn't Sophia understand my feelings?

———————

About one hundred miles away from Atlanta, it began to torrentially downpour. As rain fell against the top of the car, it sounded like someone was spraying the car with a high-pressure water hose, producing a loud, tinny noise as water slammed into metal. I switched the wiper blades to high, but to no avail. I had to slow the car's pace as I cautiously navigated the treacherous conditions rapidly developing. Looking out the windshield was like opening your eyes underwater, blurry and distorted. The only reprieve was when I occasionally passed under an overpass. In those fleeting moments, everything would stop, the windshield would clear and as soon as I was back out in the open, the noise and the pounding water resumed.

The weather violently carried on for about fifty miles and then softened to a steady flow of showering rain. I spent most of the drive battling fogged up windows and focusing on the asphalt in front of me with unshakable focus. I missed all the sites I wanted to see.

When I reached Atlanta, the sun was falling behind the horizon and lights were glowing against the dusk–colored sky. My body felt stiff, and I was starting to hallucinate with fatigue. Every so often I would jerk the steering wheel when I saw phantom shapes on the highway.

I decided against staying in another economy lodge–like motel and opted for a hotel that had a hot tub and hopefully a more comfortable bed. Not knowing where to go, I followed the freeway into the downtown area, zig zagging streets until I spotted a Home Stay Inn. We had them in Colorado, so I was familiar with the amenities.

After I checked in, I handed my suitcase over to the porter and rode the elevator up to the fourth floor and located my room. I entered the room and briefly checked it out. The room was much nicer than the Economy Lodge and rather than smelling of stale cigarettes, it smelled like freshly washed linen. The springy–clean air almost rejuvenated me, almost. I was famished from the long drive through pouring rain, so I headed back down to the lobby where I had seen a steak and chop grill. My luggage wouldn't arrive in my room for a while anyway.

I ate a particularly expensive sirloin steak, garlic mashed potatoes, and green beans. I washed the dinner down with a cold beer. My body feeling slack and slipping into food coma, I paid my bill and sauntered back up to my room.

When I entered, I was happy to see the luggage waiting for me. I was eager to find the hot tub. But first, I had to call Sophia.

As I was tired and wanting to relax, I didn't talk to Sophia long. However, my brain held on to one of her comments like a fly trap. It was persistent and challenged my thinking. When I shared the events Jennifer and I had reminisced about and Dad's attempted suicide, Sophia enlightened me with a morsel of wisdom.

After she patiently listened to me, she said, "James, some of us are Simon the Cyrenian and called to carry the cross of others who stumble. Your dad carried a heavy cross called addiction, stumbling under its weight. Like Simon the Cyrenian, you carried his heavy burdens at times and the Spirit gave you strength during those walks on the path. Through those moments you were tempered by fire." After a brief pause, she continued, "What I love about you is your tenacity and perseverance when life gets rough. I saw this when we worked together during college, and it's one of the things that makes me love you!"

Maybe Sophia was right. Maybe the hard times made me who I am today. While I mused over Sophia's words, I changed my clothes and went to the pool area on the roof.

CHAPTER FOURTEEN

T he bleach–smelling water foamed and swirled as I sat in the hot tub, euphoric with pleasure while the jets kneaded my back muscles. Every so often I rotated and adjusted my body so the jets could work on other sore muscles. When the tension began to dissipate, I sat motionlessly with my eyes closed for a while, allowing my mind to go blank.

"This sure is nice, isn't it?" said a loud booming voice.

The abrupt, barrel–sounding voice jarred me, and my eyes popped open. I saw a large man with a round head topped with receding gray hair. He had a thick, gold necklace and was holding a clear cocktail with lime wedge shoved in with the floating ice cubes. I flashed a closed mouth smile and said, "It sure is!" I hoped that would be the end of the small talk.

"Ever been ta Atlanta before?"

"No—it's my first time!"

"Where ya headed?"

"I'm on my way down to Orlando. My dad passed away."

"Aw, I am sorry!" The man shook his head and then sipped his cocktail. "I remember when my pappy died—shore tore me up. He was a mean son of a bitch and drank whiskey like Prohibition was comin', but he was a good-hearted man and taught me what was right! You know what I mean?" He didn't wait for an answer and continued, "My name's Hank, but everyone calls me Bunk." He reached extended his hand toward me.

I lifted my hand up and shook his wet, thick hand. "Nice to meet you, Bunk," I said with a smile.

"Were you close to your pappy?"

"Um—kind of. Like your pappy, he was hard-drinking, but over the past five years, we haven't spoken much," I replied. In my mind's eye, I recalled his homelessness and intermittent stays at various shelters. After the divorce from my mom, he struggled to maintain steady work or places to live.

"Hmmm, that's a shame," Bunk said while shaking his head. "Pappies are important to a boy's life. I don't mean to poke in your soup, but what happened between you two?"

Shrugging my shoulders, I said, "Nothing really happened. It was just really tough staying in touch with him because he moved around so much. Sometimes he'd get arrested and stay in jail, or sometimes he'd be out on the streets." In a mocking voice, I continued, "It's a surreal experience when you go to visit dear ol' Dad who lives in a pee–stained alley."

"Boy—you sound angry. You shouldn't be angry with your pappy! He did the best he could. That's all a pappy can do. You know what I'm sayin'?"

"I suppose—yes!"

"I bet you a C-note he took you to do things."

"He did. I can remember going to car shows and drag races with him. When he was driving a truck, I got to ride across the country with him one summer. We went to movies too."

"Now, you see there, it wasn't all bad. My pappy was a hell of a fisherman. He loved to fish. So, while I was growin' up we fished along streams. We hunted a time or two, but I sure remember fishin' with him." Bunk lifted the cocktail glass to his lips and took a sip. "I sure miss him!"

"No—it wasn't *all* bad. I have a lot of good memories of him."

"I'll bet you do! You hold on to those good memories and forget about all that other crap. Don't matter to nobody anyway. You can't change nothin' about the past. Best to hold on to a memory or two of your pappy, live your life, and enjoy yourself."

I was intrigued by Bunk's message. "You have a point there."

"Well, sure I do!" Bunk stood up in the hot tub and continued, "Well, I'm gonna get out of this kettle and go up to my room. You have a safe drive down to Orlando!"

"I will, thank you," I said. After Bunk dried off and walked out of the pool area with his drained cocktail glass, I sat in the hot tub, alone with my thoughts.

I lost track of time thinking about Bunk and Sophia. A while later I began to feel water-logged and got out of the hot tub. I dried myself off with a towel and went back to my room, fatigued by the heat.

When I lay down on the bed, the cool sheets, soft mattress, and heavy covers felt comforting against my body. I turned toward the bedside table and switched off the lamp. I was instantly asleep.

CHAPTER FIFTEEN

My eyes fluttered open. Early morning light was peeking through the white sheers hanging over the window. A ray of illumination sliced the ceiling, contrasting the darker shadows. I felt refreshed and ready to quickly get up, not because of the restful night of sleep I enjoyed, but because I would see Sophia tonight. I was eager to hit the highway.

I sat up in bed, threw the covers off my body, and rolled out of bed, firmly planting my feet on the floor. I walked into the bathroom, relieved myself, and quickly showered. Fully awakened by the hot shower, I hurriedly dressed, gathered up my belongings, and shoved them into the suitcase. After looking around the room, double-checking everything, I quickly wheeled the suitcase into the hallway, shut the door, and headed down to the lobby. The woman behind the counter was grumpy and worked very slowly. I buzzed like a live electrical wire anxious to get on the highway. It was a seven–hour drive to Orlando, and I wanted to see my girl. When I finally received my hotel receipt, it felt like history had happened and the future was writing a book about me.

I was in no mood to mess around with sit–down dining. I made a quick pitstop at a McDonald's, bought an Egg McMuffin and a tall cup of piping hot, black coffee, and sped onto the highway. I didn't even care what sites lay ahead.

As I drove, sipping my coffee, I thought about Bunk. When he referred to his dead pappy as a mean–drinking whiskey man, I thought of my maternal grandpa. When he was sober, he was the kind of guy who would give you the shirt off his back. He was devout and never missed church on Sunday. A white–out blizzard couldn't keep him away from the Lord. He was a musical prodigy who wrote songs and played several instruments. But when he started drinking whiskey, Dr. Jekyll sourly turned into Mr. Hyde. He became rage filled and insanely violent. He used to beat my grandma and get into fights with his buddies. One night he got pissed off over something at the dinner table, picked up a glass bowl filled with mashed potatoes, and hurled it at my grandma, hitting her in the head. When my mom was in seventh grade, she was standing in the kitchen after school one day, and he walked up and slapped her across the face. When she started crying and asked why he slapped her, he said, "I just wanted to test your reflexes and your memory. Let's see if you remember this a year from now!" In the throes of a week–long bender, he walked into the farm house with a shotgun and fired it over everyone's heads as they sat in the living room, blasting a crucifix hanging above the couch apart.

The stories my mom sometimes told were crazy, maybe even crazier than my stories of living with an alcoholic. I was never sure why my mom openly shared stories about my grandpa's drinking, but I suspected she wanted me to realize that addiction flows from generation to generation. When her and her siblings left home, they never wanted to be anything like my grandpa. But in the end, the boys discovered alcoholism, and the girls married men well acquainted with alcoholism.

One of my mom's commonly heard sayings was, "You are only as sick as the secrets you keep." She felt that constantly hiding the disease, not talking about it, and not confronting the problem only made it easier to continue through the family, ensuring its survival. I suppose she was right. Lucky for us, my dad's addictions were brought out at so many public events that I don't recall our lives being very secret.

I've heard of families performing interventions and confronting the addict. Some interventions are successful, and some are like trying to chop steel rebar with an axe. I wonder why it takes an intervention to make an addict quit? Wouldn't waking up the next day hung over, remembering the fact that you smashed your wife's head with a bowl, or spent the family's grocery money on cocaine be the intervention? But in the end, that's the sadness within it. The addict continues on, lost and blind, living in a bubble while everyone around them cleans up the mess, hopeful it will be the last one.

I vividly remember a time when my dad was getting out of rehab. My uncle had driven us over in his car. While my mom went inside to get him, I sat in the back seat waiting. My uncle turned around to face me and said, "Now don't cause any stress for your dad. He doesn't need any shit from you right now." Every time my mind wanders to that moment, it's as if a bolt of lightning struck my brain and caused a massive explosion of anger. I caused my dad stress?

What about the stress of riding down to the jail at midnight to bail him out? What about the stress of dragging his unconscious body out of a garage filled with carbon monoxide smoke because he thought suicide was an answer? What about the times his paychecks were spent on cocaine instead of groceries or rent? What about the missed birthdays and embarrassing drunkenness in front of my friends? And he had the nerve to tell me not to give my dad stress?

Lost in my thoughts, I began to feel urinary pressure from the morning's coffee. When I spotted an exit leading to a gas station, I pulled off the highway. As I approached the gas station, I noticed an old Ford station wagon, faded from years of sun sitting on the shoulder with a flat back tire. A black woman wearing a flowery sundress with a white headband was standing outside the car in the hot sun.

I pulled onto the shoulder, parked my car behind the Ford, and got out and walked toward her. The humidity instantly dampened my clothes and made my skin feel clammy.

"Do you need any help?" I asked.

"Why, yes! It was kind of you to stop," the woman replied.

"My name is James," I said, reaching my hand toward her.

"Thelma," she said, shaking my hand.

I noticed two small children, a boy and a girl on their knees in the backseat watching me.

"Do you have a spare tire?"

"Well, I was just about to figure that out." She winked and flashed a warm smile.

I judged the station wagon to be pretty old. "Um—I'll bet the spare is tucked under a trap door or mat in the back of station wagons like this one. Should we look?"

"Sure!" Thelma walked toward the back of the car. As she approached, I had to back up to let her pass. As she grabbed the rear door handle, she said, "I see you have Colorado plates. Are you on a road trip somewhere?"

"Yes, I'm driving to Orlando. Uh, my dad died a few days ago."

"Oh—I'm sorry for your loss! Losing a parent is hard."

"Thank you," I mumbled.

With the rear door open, Thelma rummaged in the back and lifted up a mat and with a muffled voice, said, "Yep, the spare tire is back here!" She straightened her back and turned toward me. "It looks heavy!"

Laughing, I said, "No problem, I'll get it out." As Thelma stepped aside, I walked to the rear of the car, lifted the mat with one hand and grabbed the center of the spare with the other, hauling it out of the car. I rolled it to the side of the car and laid it on the ground. I walked back to the rear of the car and searched for a jack and tire iron. Once I found them, I carried them to the side of the car. While I positioned the old jack against the car's rear bumper, Thelma stood behind me overseeing my work.

"My grandma passed away a while back. Mm-mm, she was a sweet woman, and I loved her dearly. I remember sitting on her lap while she told me stories about her family and growin' up in Alabama. Some of her stories were funny, some were sad, and some of them plum scared me stiff. Bless her heart, she always had a lesson or two buried in them stories she told. James, are you a bible man?"

As I wrenched the lug nuts off, I grunted, "Sort of. I was raised Catholic and went to church every Sunday."

"Well, then you might be familiar with one of Jesus' famous parables. He said, 'Remove the wooden beam from your eye first; then you will see clearly to remove the splinter from your brother's eye.' I reckon that's a fancy way of telling us to not judge others. When my grandma was called home to Jesus, folks from all over showed up. Some wanted to pay their respects, and others were looking for money she might have left behind. But what bothered me most was the way folks stood around passin' judgement on her life and how she lived. James—these were bible-carrying believers who somehow forgot the words of Jesus. It's not for us to stand around judging the lives of others. That's Jesus' job. We just gotta worry about savin' our own souls!"

"Thelma, I suppose you're right. I can remember my mother telling me to never speak ill of the dead."

"Your mama spoke rightly. It's not right to speak ill of the dead. But it ain't right to judge people no how. You gotta let people be." In the corner of my eye, I could see Thelma waving her arms animatedly.

I laughed inwardly as Thelma preached the pulpit behind me. It was a strange, out-of-the-blue message. With the spare securely bolted to the car, I carried the flat tire to the rear of the car and laid it under the mat. I gathered the jack and lug wrench and placed them alongside the flat tire. Turning toward Thelma, I said, "Well, you're all set. Hopefully that will last until you can find a tire store."

Thelma walked toward me, threw her long skinny arms around me, and said, "James, bless your heart for stopping to help me. You have a safe drive down to Orlando!"

"You're welcome," I said, withdrawing from Thelma's embrace. I walked over to my Mustang, opened the door, sat down in the driver's seat, and closed the door. The car was stifling hot and the air felt thick and heavy. My lower stomach pained me as the urinary urge pushed outward. I fired the engine up and quickly drove to the gas station.

CHAPTER SIXTEEN

After relieving myself, I replenished the gas tank and followed a curvy frontage road back to the highway. The sun was intense, and I switched the car's air conditioner to high, vainly hoping to vanquish the hot, sticky, humid heat. As I looked out the windshield, I noticed fields of brownish-green grass on both sides of the highway dotted with yellow flowers and isolated groups of large green bushes. The highway's asphalt was light gray with black lines snaking across where road crews filled in cracks with tar.

As I listened to the Eagles, my cell phone rang.

"Hi James," Sophia said.

"Hi," I said in a happy voice.

"Can you talk?"

"Yes—but make it quick. I only have a couple hundred minutes left on my cell phone this month and I'll need them in Orlando."

Sighing in frustration, Sophia said, "James, you are so frugal. If you run out, you can just buy more."

"It's that spendy attitude that scares me," I teased.

"For richer or poorer James. If you are poor, I will still love you!" Sophia chuckled in the phone.

"When I'm poor, you'll just find a man with more sugar," I playfully joked.

"Oy vey—I will always love you. . . even if you are a homeless vagabond begging for spare change!"

Smiling, I said, "Then I am the luckiest man in the world! So, what did you need—before my minutes run out?"

"Don't worry about finding a hotel or picking me up at the airport. I booked two rooms at the Hilton Orlando." In a hesitant voice, she concluded with, "It was a good deal, and I couldn't wait."

"That sounds good. I trust your judgement. I'll head straight to the hotel when I get in town."

"Okay, that sounds good James. *Muah-muah*, I'll see you soon!"

"I'll see you soon!" Smiling, I hung up the phone and refocused my attention on the highway.

As I drove, I passed under a thick, emerald–green canopy of trees. Sunlight poked through the shadowy reflections of interlaced tree branches as they moved across the Mustang's hood. Sometimes beauty is all around us and we are driving too fast to see it.

Sophia often says I am endearing, but in truth she has always been the endearing one. Life would be dark and gloomy without her. In many ways she has become my guiding angel, serving as a constant catalyst in my life, pushing me forward, even when I am resistant. In a weird way, she is like Mary at the Wedding Feast of Cana, pushing a resistant Jesus and then trusting he will perform the miracle. Of course, I certainly fall short of performing any miracles. In fact, I think I've fallen short of walking in the path of Jesus too many times. Listening isn't the hard part, it's the "doing" that trips us up.

Thinking of Sophia, I felt a stirring within me.

CHAPTER SEVENTEEN

The sun was beginning its elliptical slide downward when I arrived in Orlando. The light gray freeway had widened into four lanes, and palm trees lined the sides. Green and white signage directing sightseers to Universal Studios, Disney World, and SeaWorld began to appear. Along with the signage, red taillights began to appear as I approached the slow-moving rush-hour traffic. I eased up on the throttle and began to slow the Mustang's speed.

After a few miles of tiresome traffic moving slower than molasses poured from a jar, I located the Hilton Orlando. Architecturally, it was a large L-shaped building with small glass windows inside of larger squares, creating a visual illusion that looked like windows inside of windows. In front of the hotel were foliage-filled gardens, palm trees, terraced wading pools surrounded by lounge chairs, and large rocks with gushing waterfalls.

While mesmerized by the hotel's luxurious beauty, I was financially appalled. What on earth was Sophia thinking? As I contemplated the hotel's nightly costs, I felt my wallet flee my back pocket and run away. Maybe this is where my life of panhandling would begin.

I hesitantly parked the Mustang, unloaded my luggage, and walked to the hotel lobby, fumbling with my belongings along the way. At the far end of the lobby, I saw a long black counter with under-lights illuminating the front–facing maple colored panels. Impeccably shiny white marble floors stretched across the area with periodic squares of blue and red floral–patterned carpet hosting small couches, chairs, and small working tables. As I approached the concierge's desk, a short woman with tawny-colored skin and black hair said, "Good afternoon. How may I help you?"

"Uh—my fiancée Sophia Villanueva reserved two rooms —I'm not sure if they're under my name or hers. I am James Fisher."

Smiling brightly, the woman said, "Sure. Let me look on the computer here. How do you spell her last name?"

"V-I-L-L-A-N-U-E-V-A," I slowly said.

The woman punched in the letters on here keyboard and waited a few seconds. "Oh, yes—she reserved two rooms. In the notes, it says to assign the rooms together if possible and to send you to your room if you arrived first."

That was music to my ears. A long, piping–hot shower was desperately needed before I saw Sophia. "Great. What do you need from me?"

"I need to see a photo ID and a credit card to keep on file in case you order room service or movies in your room."

"That's fine." I fished my wallet out of my back pocket, opened it, and pulled out my driver's license and credit card. Handing them to the woman, I said, "Here you go."

The woman set the two cards on a ledge under her screen and quickly tapped the keys below. After a few moments, she handed the cards back to me and briefly smiled. Then she quickly turned and walked over to printer that began to spit out sheets of paper. When she collected the printouts, she came back to the desk and laid them on the counter in front of me. "Please read and sign the two documents at the bottom."

Not bothering to read the documents, I signed them and spun them around on the countertop. "Here you go," I said.

The woman grabbed the documents, prepared an electronic key, and placed it into a booklet where she wrote the room number on the front. "Okay, you're all set." Pointing to the left of the desk, she said, "The elevators are over there. Just go up to the fourth floor, turn right, and walk down the hall. The room will be on the right."

"Excellent. Thank you!" I said. Smiling, I walked up to the room with my key. A porter had already taken my luggage while I was at the counter.

The directions I was provided led me straight to the room. When I entered, my luggage was parked between a plush queen bed and a dark wood desk. The room was elegant but simple, featuring blue and beige carpeting, a walnut armoire with an LCD TV, a bedside stand, and a reading chair with foot stool in the corner.

I opened my luggage and retrieved the travel bag with bathroom necessities. I peeled off my clothes and walked into the bathroom where I took a long, steamy shower. Refreshed from my shower, I lay on the top of my bed, intending to take a nap when my cell phone rang.

"Hey, Mom!"

"I was talking to Jennifer, and she told me you are driving down to Orlando."

"Yes—I wanted some time to myself to process some things."

"What's going on? Anything you want to talk about?"

"Mom, it's a few things. Sophia and I had an argument over children again. Because of that, I've been thinking about Dad a lot and remembering some of the crazy things that happened over the years. And I feel like Dad's sudden death left things unresolved."

"What do you mean by unresolved?"

"Well—I feel like I barely saw him over the last few years. He was supposed to be coming out to Colorado, and now that opportunity is gone. We just never really talked about things. There are so many things I wish I could have asked him."

"Like what?"

"Like when did the train go off the tracks? I mean, when did his life of addiction begin? I remember bits and pieces of Grandma and Grandpa saying what a hellion he was as a kid." I paused to collect my thoughts. "Do you think Grandma and Grandpa might have done things differently if they'd known how his life turned out?"

"I don't know. It was a different time back then. Problems were not discussed but rather swept under the rug. People didn't talk about addictions, and you certainly didn't want anyone to know if there was an alcohol problem in your family. There were many family secrets. They didn't have the resources we have today to recognize and deal with addictions. When he got into trouble, they fixed things. I remember one time when he got thrown in jail, he called them and asked if they would bail him out. He gave your grandpa a sob story about how he was going to lose his job. I told your grandpa to just leave him in jail, and maybe he'd get a wakeup call. But Grandpa felt sorry for him and bailed him out despite my opinions. A week later he lost that job anyway. I don't think they ever understood that sometimes tough love was what he needed. They just did the best they knew how to do at that time."

"Wow—I never knew that! But I think Grandma did regret things later in life. I remember when I visited her in the hospital while she was dying and how she squeezed my hand and said, 'Don't you become like your dad! You go make something of your life.' I never forgot that. When I think of them, and think of Dad, I wonder if I will do the right things with my future kids. You know?"

Mom chuckled. "Jamie, parenting isn't something we can plan out. Kids don't come with instruction manuals, and every child is different. What works for one child may not work for the next child. You kind of figure it out as you go—situation by situation. Your grandparents made decisions based upon their time and the circumstances in front of them. Your dad made his choices. He made the choice to start drinking and doing drugs. But then, it no longer became a choice. The addiction took over his life, and he couldn't see his way out."

"Hmmm." There was silence while I processed mom's comment.

"Jamie—as far as kids are concerned, you will make a wonderful parent. You are nothing like your father."

"Yeah, but what about my college years? I started to follow in his footsteps. . ."

"Yes—you went through a rebellious stage. There were a few turbulent years, but the difference is you realized you were making bad choices, and you turned things around. You chose not to go down that same path. You took responsibility for your actions. You turned your life around and worked very hard to maintain good grades. That's the difference between you and your dad. He never wanted to take responsibility for his actions."

Resigned, I commented, "Yeah, I guess that's true." After a pause, I laughed. "I would have made a bad drug addict anyway. I really didn't like being high, and drugs made me feel stupid."

"Jamie, please don't let your dad's life and the bad choices he made dictate what your life will be. You have a lot of wisdom for your age, and I am very proud of you. See, you are asking the questions and thinking all this through. That's a real sign of maturity and wisdom. You are going to be just fine, and you will raise healthy children." Mom laughed and said, "Your problem is you think too much.

I felt uplifted. Conversations with my mom always felt therapeutic. "So—I went to see Tommy the other day. He's still angry with me."

"Give your brother time. He is struggling in life and sees you doing better than he is. Some of it's jealousy."

"I suppose. I've tried to help him, but like Dad, there are no boundaries or appreciation."

"Well, he's not in a place to appreciate your help right now. He is sick and caught up in his own life. Addiction is a very selfish disease."

"Funny that you said disease. Do you think there is a genetic element—like it's something that flows from generation to generation? I mean, look at Tommy! He turned out just like Dad."

"Yes, it does seem to flow from generation to generation. Your grandfather was an alcoholic, as you know. My brothers Robbie and Denny became alcoholics. Jonathan and Jeremy started down that path, but the threat of losing their wives and kids were strong deterrents, and they chose to turn their lives around. Two of my sisters and I married men who became alcoholics, so yes, I believe the tendencies are there, but the choices we make ultimately will determine the outcome. I believe education about addiction is very important, especially when you come from a family where addiction is prevalent. And addiction needs to be confronted head on. You have heard me say you are only as sick as the secrets you keep. You can't hide or run away from the problem. Sometimes you need tough love and intervention when a loved one is headed down that path."

"You confronted Dad, and he never changed!"

"Honey, I waited too long. I put up with his drinking and drugging for longer than I should have. If I had a chance to do some things over, I would have confronted his behavior earlier in our marriage. But I didn't know better. I became as sick as he was. Alcoholism not only affects the alcoholic, but the family as well."

I remembered my grandpa's raging alcoholism and some of my mom's crazy stories. "I remember some of the things you told me about grandpa and how he once fired a shotgun in the house."

"Shoot, he did crazier things than that!"

"Like what?"

Mom paused for a moment. "Well, there was the time he ran us off the road."

"What? What do you mean he ran you off the road?"

"Jamie, it's a long story!"

"Mom, I've got time. And besides, you can't just drop a bombshell like that and not tell me. I want to hear the story."

"Hmm. Okay. It was a hot dusty day in the fall of 1962. Daddy was drinking heavy and had been fighting with Mama all day. In mid-afternoon, Mama left the farm to go pick up me, Jonathan, Maggie, and Denny from school. Daddy got mad at Mama for leaving and followed her into town. When he was drinking, he just couldn't let a fight go.

"When school let out, me and Jonathan climbed into Mama's yellow convertible Studebaker, and Maggie and Denny got into Daddy's old Hudson. Daddy followed Mama as she drove back to the farm, angrily ramming her car from behind. Each time his Hudson hit us, we lurched forward, whiplashing my head into the seat.

We were driving down a dusty dirt road and just as we approached the bridge crossing the Platte river, Daddy rammed us really hard, causing our car to fishtail and go off an embankment and flip over. As the car lay upside down, Mama was screaming, asking if Jonathan and I were okay. My leg was bleeding really bad, but I lied and said I was fine. It was a sheer miracle we weren't killed. When Jonathan tried to pry the passenger–side door open, he realized it was stuck in the thick mud, so he kicked the window until it busted out. We were all able to crawl out of the car.

"Daddy never stopped. He kept on driving home while Maggie and Denny screamed at him in the car. When they reached the farm, Maggie jumped out of the car and called the police.

The police came to check on us, and when they realized we were okay they drove us back to the farm. Daddy was still in a rage and tried to sic our collie on the police, which would have been like Tommy siccing Lassie on the mailman. She was a sweet, loving dog.

"The police hauled Daddy to jail."

"That's crazy!"

"Yes, it was!" Mom laughed and said, "I wonder how I am even sane!"

I laughed. "Mom, your stories are as crazy as mine!

Okay, to my point—how can I know if the disease will flow to my kids or not? I mean, Jennifer and I made it through things, and Tommy became a total drug fiend!"

Mom breathed in deeply. "Jamie, you can't live in fear of what might or might not happen. Every kid is different, and circumstances affect them differently. You and Jennifer found maturity and determination within the turmoil. Tommy got lost. None of us ever knows how things will turn out. God has a plan for all of us, and you just have to trust!"

Sophia said the same stuff to me. "Yeah, I suppose you're right." I was resigned to that thought. God's plan might be that one of my kids is an addict, and I will have to live through it.

"Honey, I need to run. Call me if you need to talk some more."

"I will, Mom. I'm glad you called."

"Me too. Love you!"

The phone went dead.

The call with my mom left me tired. I took a power-generating nap until I was awoken by the cell phone ringing.

"Hello," I said in a tired, sluggish voice.

"Hi, James, it's Sophia," a familiar, sweet-sounding voice said.

"Oh, hi. I was just lying down for a nap," I said rubbing my left eye and inhaling deeply through my nose.

"I'm just giving you a quick call to let you know my plane landed, and once I get my luggage, I'll grab a cab and come to the hotel. Did you get checked in okay?"

"Yes—it was super easy. I'm not completely sure if the rooms are side by side, but I got the feeling they already had things set up."

"They should have. When I called, they said reserving two rooms next to each other would be no problem. Can you call the restaurant up on the roof and reserve a table for two? Um—just to be safe, make it for 6:30. I just need to freshen up, and then I'll be ready to go."

"Sure," I said. In a poorly Italian–accented voice, I teased, "For my lady, a table for two by the window!"

"Your accent is awful. Maybe our honeymoon should be in Italy so you can improve it," Sophia joked.

"For you, anything," I continued in my bad accent.

"Looks like my luggage is coming out of the carousel. I'll see you soon," Sophia hurriedly said. The line went dead.

CHAPTER EIGHTEEN

After I spoke with Sophia, I called the rooftop restaurant and made a 6:30 p.m. reservation for two. Business attended to, I gathered a couple of pillows, fluffed them, and propped them against the headboard. I scooted into an upright, seated position, grabbed the remote and switched on the TV. I absent-mindedly flipped through the channels until I discovered an old favorite, *Back to the Future*. I smiled inwardly as Christopher Lloyd said, "When this baby hits eighty-eight miles per hour, you're gonna see some serious shit." Instantly, I felt cozied and warm, losing my thoughts and troubles to Marty McFly's historical adventures.

The cell phone began ringing in the middle of the scene where Marty wakes up in bed, lying on his stomach in last night's clothes with the song "Back in Time" playing. Disappointed by the interruption, I answered it.

"Hello," I said.

"Hey Jamie, its Jennifer," said my sister's familiar voice.

"Hey, what's going on?" I inquired.

"So—I'm flying in later tonight with Vincent and the kids. In fact, we're waiting in the terminal now." A woman's voice announced a departing flight to Toledo that sounded echoed, like a PA system announcement in a large empty room. "Detective Daniels from the Orlando Police Department called and said the police investigation located a suspect and the coroner's report is complete, so they are releasing his body."

"What?" I said incredulously. When I glanced over to the bedside table, I noticed the clock said 6:00 p.m. "Shit—can I call you right back? I am supposed to meet Sophia for dinner in a half hour!"

"Sure," Jennifer said with a surprised voice. "Call me right back."

I hung up the phone and called Sophia, telling her Jennifer needed to talk with me about my dad and to go ahead and get the table. I'd be there as soon as I was off the phone.

I dialed Jennifer's phone number. When she answered, I said, "Okay, sorry about that—you were saying Dad was murdered?"

"Yeah, I guess the coroner's report determined the gash in his head was consistent with blunt–force trauma. They discovered motel footage showing a known drug dealer going into the hotel and leaving around the time of the murder."

Feeling sick to my stomach, I mumbled out, "I can't believe it—so what does this mean?"

"Well, it sounds like it has turned into a murder investigation, but from what Detective Daniels said, it sounds like it's an open–and–shut case. All the evidence points to the dealer. He said since the coroner's report is released, there wasn't any reason why we couldn't arrange services."

I was knotted inside. I hated the idea of our dad dying in a violent way. "So, should we go down to the funeral home tomorrow? What about a church?"

"I work with a lady who is from Orlando. She recommended Our Lady of Lourdes. I'll meet you at the funeral home at nine. Can you look up the church?"

How is it possible my dad's death became as chaotic as his life? It was like a proverbial baker adding bits of chocolate to an already sweet frosting. "Yes. And nine sounds good."

"Jamie, I don't want to keep you. Go enjoy your dinner with Sophia. I'll call you in the morning."

"Okay. Is there anything else I should do?"

"No, go eat. We'll sort this out tomorrow."

Internally, I felt like I should be doing something. This news was upsetting and knotted my insides. "Call me as soon as you are up!"

"Will do. Give Sophia a hug for me. I can't wait to see her!"

Smiling, I said, "I will. Have a safe flight."

"Thanks." The line went dead.

CHAPTER NINETEEN

As I approached the restaurant's entrance, I could see Sophia's long curly, black hair from behind. My senses were so finely tuned to Sophia that I could spot her in the center of a Hong Kong street mob. The restaurant was dimly lit. Glass centerpieces with flickering candles adorned round tables draped with white tablecloths.

I briefly exchanged a greeting with the maître d', explaining that my fiancée was already seated and awaiting my arrival. With my eyes focused upon Sophia, I walked past the maître d's wooden podium and headed toward our table.

As I approached, I lightly touched Sophia's shoulder. Startled, she swiveled her head sideways and when she saw me in the corner of her eye, she stood from her chair, turning to face me.

Sophia's face was as refreshing as an ice–cold lemonade on a hot and dry summer day. While my eyes drank in the sight of her beauty, I extended my arms and she longingly fell into them. Her embrace was warm and comforting.

We had only been apart for three days, but it felt much longer. I held her tenderly against my body, smelling the scent of shampoo in her damp hair, feeling the softness of her face against mine. Two hearts rejoined, beating as one again.

Breathing in deeply, I released her from my embrace, letting my hands lightly graze the sides of her arms. As I stepped back, I noticed cherry–red lipstick contrasting against her olive skin and a dazzling burgundy dress brightening her brown eyes.

Stepping to the side and moving toward my chair, I said, "How was your flight?"

"Quiet. The roughest part was rush–hour traffic on my way to DIA," she said, sitting back into her chair.

"Good," I commented while pulling my chair out and sitting down. I noticed a mahogany bar deeper into the restaurant, backdropped by a mirror faintly lit by overhead lights. Liquor bottles were prominently displayed on shelves and a big, black cash register was nestled in the middle of the back wall. "Did they have our rooms together?"

Sophia's slight smile suggested I asked a dumb question.

"Yes—I would have stopped by, but you were talking with Jennifer," she replied, her voice betraying disappointment.

"I'm sorry about that. She was at the airport and in a hurry to talk with me. Otherwise I would have called her back. She said to tell you hi, by the way." I smiled.

Sophia softened and asked, "So, what is going on?" with a concerned look on her face.

Leaning back and sighing heavily, I said, "Well, the police concluded he was murdered by a drug dealer." My eyes teared up as I uttered those words.

Sophia reached her hand across the table, taking my

hand in hers. "Oh, James, I'm sorry! What do the police think happened?"

I wiped my right cheek. "I'm not sure. The police didn't share any of the details." I wasn't sure I wanted to know the gory details.

"Oh, my gosh, that's awful. Are you okay?" Sophia's face held a look of concern and she squeezed my hand tighter.

Shrugging my shoulders, I said, "I think I am in shock. I honestly don't know what to feel right now. Why did he have to go out like that?"

Releasing my hand, Sophia leaned back in her chair. "Sometimes we never know these things, James."

Resigned to circumstances, I said, "I guess not."

Abruptly we were interrupted when a waiter appeared at our table, setting small white plates before us and placing a platter of bread rolls on our table. He was tall, with short black hair parted on the side and wore black rimmed glasses. He was wearing black dress pants with a black, pocketed apron tied behind him, a black shirt, and a red tie.

"Can I get you something to drink? Perhaps wine or a cocktail?" the waiter asked Sophia.

"I will have a glass of your house merlot," Sophia replied.

"And for you, sir?"

"I will have the same," I replied.

"Very well, I will get them ordered," the waiter said, turning from our table and walking away.

While we waited for the waiter to return, Sophia and I each reached for a dark rye bread roll from the platter. Simultaneously, we broke open the rolls and buttered them with herb butter.

"So, what are you and Jennifer going to do?" Sophia asked, moving a piece of bread to her mouth.

As she posed her question, I had taken a bite of my food and was chewing. After I swallowed, I replied, "Well, we will meet with the funeral home first and figure out how to get his body cremated."

What about a funeral? You have to wait on that? James, you should at least have a mass said for him." Sophia took another bite.

"That reminds me. Jennifer said a co-worker suggested a parish called Our Lady of Lourdes. Can you chase that down for us? That would be super helpful!"

Flushing with appreciation, Sophia replied, "Yes, I am happy to help."

Just as Sophia and I were finishing our first bread rolls, the waiter arrived at our table carrying a round tray with two small carafes of wine and two wine glasses. While balancing the tray with one hand, the waiter flipped the wine glasses over and set them before us on the table. Then he poured one carafe into Sophia's glass and the other carafe of merlot into mine. "Is the wine satisfactory?"

Sophia and I swirled the wine in our glasses like we were professionals from Napa Valley and individually sipped the wine.

"Yes, the wine is good," I said.

"Very good," Sophia said.

With a look of satisfaction on his face, the waiter said, "Very well, are you ready to order?" The waiter gestured toward the menus with one hand while holding his other hand against his abdomen.

Looking at Sophia who nodded in agreement, I said, "No, can you give us a minute?"

"Absolutely!" The waiter smiled and slowly walked away.

Turning my head after watching the waiter walk away, I

grabbed my glass of wine and raised it up. "A toast to you my soon–to–be wife. You are my soul mate, my confidant, and my best friend. A journey without you beside me isn't a journey worth taking!"

Holding her glass of wine up, Sophia responded. "A toast to the love of my life—you are the man I want to spend my life with, in sickness, in health, for richer or poorer."

Sophia and I adoringly smiled at each other, clinked our glasses, and took a drink of wine.

Setting my glass on the table, I said, "I am happy you are here with me. I couldn't have dealt with this without you!"

With a tender look on her face, Sophia said, "I am always here for you!"

We each sat in silence, facing each other for a while.

Changing the subject and tone of her voice, she inquired, "So how was your trip—do you feel any different?"

My mind quickly reviewed the road trip, my life experiences, Sophia's comments about stumbling when we disobey God and Simon the Cyrenian, the discussion with Bunk, and Thelma's bible sermon. "I feel like I am making peace with the past." In my mind's eye, I recalled my dad's hazel eyes and smile. "I think he did the best he could, and I don't believe he meant to do harm. He just got lost in addiction, and we got caught in his wake. There is some truth to what you said about disobeying God's plan for us and pursuing our own desires. In the end we fail, and sadly, I don't think anyone ever pointed that out to him. But—I realized that I learned from his mistakes in many ways."

Sophia's eyes twinkled and her cheek bones became

prominent as she smiled. Finishing my sentence, Sophia said, "And seeing those mistakes, you can live a better life!" I knew what she was hinting at.

In the corner of my eye I saw the waiter approaching. "Have you decided on dinner?" the waiter asked.

Abruptly picking up my menu, I said, "Uh—I'll have the uh—filet mignon with baked potato and grilled asparagus."

"Excellent choice sir. How would you like that cooked?

"Medium-rare."

"And what would you like on your salad?"

"Blue cheese."

Nodding his head in agreement, the waiter said, "Excellent choice, sir, and for the lady?"

Sophia's eyes darted back and forth as she quickly read the menu. "Um—I'll have the petite filet and shrimp."

"How would you like the filet cooked?"

"Well done."

"And for your salad?"

"Blue cheese as well."

"Excellent. I will get those started right away." The waiter tucked his pad of paper and pen into his front apron pocket and walked toward the kitchen.

As the waiter walked away, I turned my head to the side toward the windows. I could see the reflection of other patrons seated at the round dinner tables. A brightly lighted Ferris wheel stood in the distance. The yellow and neon pink lights contrasted against the darkened sky. I thought of my paternal grandparents and my dad. "Sophia—listen, I know you want kids, but I'm still not sure. Even if I learned from my dad's mistakes, there is no guarantee my kids would be okay. Addiction seems to get passed down through generations. There are alcoholics on both sides of my family. My mom's dad was an alcoholic, and some of her siblings became alcoholics. My great-grandpa Fisher was a binging alcoholic. My dad was an alcoholic, and of course you know about my brother Tommy." I took a sip of water. "Sophia—I don't know if you ever knew this, but I got mixed up with alcohol and drugs during my college years. . ."

"James, I did know it! It wasn't that hard to figure out, and you were kind of out there." Sophia flashed a playful smile. "But we all were. Back when we met, I was an activist and belonged to a few political groups. I am ashamed to admit it now, but I even marched for pro-choice one time. We were both experimenting and figuring out who we were. That's what college kids do. I'm no more a political activist than you are an alcoholic. You changed yourself, and I believe you are truly different from other people."

I was surprised Sophia knew I was messed up. "A pro-choice activist—really?" I said with a look of incredulousness.

Sophia ignored my question. "You have to follow your heart, James." The brightness in Sophia's face contorted to a look of sadness and hurt. "I am patient, James, and in my heart, I believe you will find the answers you are searching for. But if we get to our wedding day and you still refuse to have children, I will have to break it off. I love you more than you know, but I want children, and if you will not give them to me, then. . ." She shrugged her shoulders.

The thought of losing Sophia tore at my heart. But I couldn't overcome my fear. "You can't mean that!"

"I'm sorry—but I do!"

In a vain attempt to lighten the mood, I joked, "Couldn't I interest you in a nice poodle? They don't wake you up at midnight to breastfeed. They don't require poopy diaper changes or write on the wall with crayons, and they don't turn into smart–ass teenagers and sneak out."

Her face betraying amusement, Sophia said, "Cute, James! I want children—a boy and a girl. . . no poodle. We can get a golden retriever when the kids are older."

"I'll think on it. The golden retriever I mean."

With a maleficent chuckle, she shot back, "I'm serious. You better figure it out."

With nowhere to go, I changed the subject. "Well, since we are already here, what do you think of visiting Universal Studios tomorrow? I've always wanted to see Mel's Drive-In. If my dad were with us, he would have loved that. Plus, it would be a good opportunity to spend quality time with Jennifer's family!"

The waiter arrived with a folded wooden stand in one arm and a tray filled with two plates in the other. With a quick jerk of his hand, the stand expanded, and he set it down. He lowered the tray filled with plates and set it on top of the stand. "For the lady, petite filet with shrimp." He set a plate down in front of Sophia. "For you, sir, the filet mignon." He placed my dinner in front of me. "May I get you anything else?"

Glancing at Sophia, I answered, "No, I think we're good for now."

"Very well." The waiter scooped up the tray and stand and walked away from our table.

Sophia and I enjoyed our meal and planned some fun excursions while we were in Orlando. After dinner we strolled hand in hand among the hotel's gardens which emanated a spicy fragrance. The night air felt warm and muggy against my skin. Later, we shared a kiss and long embrace before we retreated to our hotel rooms.

CHAPTER TWENTY

The mud was thick and gooey as I crawled on my hands and knees, struggling to move forward. The sky was light gray as if I was part of an old black–and–white movie. With each movement forward, I could feel my body sinking as my fingers dug into the wet, heavy mud, clawing for a firm hold. In the distance, I saw a sinister–looking man. He was standing, laughing at me as I crawled. The laugh was an evil, taunting sneer. A surge of anger rippled through my body as I screamed, "Why won't you help me?" The man continued to laugh, seeming to enjoy my struggle.

Fade to black.

The ocean water was the shade of cold steel. Violent waves raged around me as I flailed my arms, struggling to stay afloat. Sharks menacingly swam around me, circling. I was afraid for my life as I struggled to stay afloat in the raging ocean. Suddenly, a large whale burst from underneath the waves and swallowed me. I felt the thrash of a spongy whale tongue and saw a cavernous space with bone–like ridges arching across. I was trapped and sure to be dead.

I abruptly awoke, sweating and disoriented. As my eyes scanned the room, I realized I was in my hotel room. The visions of the man laughing and the whale chomping faded as I lay on my back groggy from a night of fitful sleep. It was just a nightmare, not real, I told myself.

Daylight had broken, and the sun's rays poked through the edge of the curtains. Rubbing my eyes, I threw the covers off of my body, rolled off the bed, and stood on the floor. I sluggishly walked into the bathroom, pulled the plastic off a drinking glass, and filled it with tap water. I gulped down the water and turned on the shower, letting the water warm up. After I tested the water with my hands a few times, I peeled off my clothes and stepped in, hoping to wash the bad dreams out of my head.

Feeling refreshed from the shower, I dressed in a pair of khaki shorts and a flowery Hawaiian shirt. Not bothering to put socks or sandals on, I shoved the room key card into my pocket, walked out of the room, and stopped at Sophia's door. I knocked lightly and waited.

Sophia pulled the door open and said, "Good morning!"

I noticed she was already dressed and wearing a pair of white shorts and a black tank top. "Oh—you're dressed already? I was worried I might wake you if I called your room."

"I couldn't sleep. I had nightmares all night and kept waking up."

"Me too. There must have been something in the air."

"Must have."

"Are you hungry?"

"Coffee sounds good right now. Where do you want to go?"

"Let's see what's close by. Do you feel like walking?"

"Um—sure. Let me put on some sandals and grab my purse." Looking at my bare feet, she continued, "Are you going without shoes?"

I chuckled. "No, I'll be right back." I quickly walked back to my hotel room. Just as I was heading back out the door wearing my sandals, Sophia was standing in the hallway.

"Ready?"

"Yes—let's go."

We walked out of the hotel and strolled through the front gardens. They looked much different in the daylight. I could hear the faint whooshing sound of a waterfall. Meandering through curvy paths, we located a busy street and walked alongside it until we came upon a little diner called Trixie's.

The hostess quickly seated us in a booth toward the front of the diner. I could hear the clink of dishes echoing from the kitchen.

CHAPTER TWENTY-ONE

A waitress dressed in a pink and white 1950s style dress brought a pitcher of coffee and two glasses to our table. "Good morning!" she said in a chipper voice.

"Good morning." Sophia's voice sounded sluggish.

"Coffee to get you started—and here are some menus. I'll give you a minute to decide."

"Thank you," I said with appreciation.

Sophia and I individually filled our mugs with coffee. I drank mine black and Sophia ruined hers with powdered cream.

After sipping my coffee for a few minutes, I broke the silence. "I had these crazy dreams last night and I just can't shake the images. In one, I was crawling on my hands and knees through thick mud while an evil looking guy laughed at me, and in the other, I was flailing in a raging ocean when a whale swallowed me."

Sophia chuckled. "Well, I can't interpret dreams, but getting swallowed by a whale reminds me of the story of Jonah and the whale."

"Jonah and the whale?"

"Yes. I'm sure you read the bible story of Jonah when you were a kid, right?"

"Refresh my memory. I can't remember how it went."

"Well, Jonah disobeys God's call to deliver a prophecy to Nineveh and boards a ship to a foreign city. God becomes angry with Jonah and stirs the ocean up around the ship. Afraid for their lives, the men cast Jonah overboard hoping his God will relent. God then sends a whale to devour Jonah, and he spends three days and three nights in the belly of the whale repenting for his disobedience. God relents and commands the whale to spit Jonah out on dry land." Sophia paused while she took a sip of her coffee. With a twinkle in her eye, she said, "Are you disobeying God?" Her face shifted to a look of concern. "No, seriously, James, is there something that's bothering you?"

Not wanting to get into this conversation with Sophia right now, I shrugged and said, "No not really. . ." But in my mind, I started wondering if these dreams had something to do with the internal struggle I was having about not wanting children. Was an evil spirit taunting me as I wrestled this decision in my mind?

As Sophia and I were finishing our breakfast, Jennifer called.

"Good morning," she said.

"Good morning! We are just finishing up breakfast," I said.

"We just ate as well. Vincent is going to take the kids down to the pool while we meet with the funeral home."

"That sounds like a good idea. Did you still want to meet at nine?" I confirmed.

"Uh—Yes. I forgot to give you the address yesterday. It's 555 Everglade Boulevard."

"Hang on. . . Sophia, do you have a pen?" After Sophia fished a pen from her purse and handed it to me, I started writing the address on a napkin. "555 Everglade Boulevard —is that right?"

"Yes. Be there by nine?"

"I'll try to be. Hopefully it's not too hard to find."

"Yes."

"Okay, I'll see you in a bit then."

"Sounds good."

After we finished our breakfast, Sophia and I walked back to the hotel. We both went up to our rooms where I quickly retrieved my car keys, and Sophia called Our Lady of Lourdes.

Finding the funeral home ended up being an adventure. I got lost three times and kept stopping to ask people for directions. I think the first two were screwing with me. Thankfully, I found the funeral home with fifteen minutes to spare.

Right as I was climbing out of the Mustang, I saw Jennifer pulling up in blue Chevy Cobalt. Upon seeing me, she quickened her pace and parked alongside.

Jennifer got out of her car and walked over to me, beaming a large smile. She looked just as I remembered, long brown hair, green eyes, pouty lips, and to my annoyance, an inch taller than me. I have always felt her height was proof of God's sense of humor.

Smiling broadly, I reached my arms toward her and said, "Hey, sis—long time, not enough see!"

Jennifer extended her arms and hugged me tightly. "Likewise. Why don't you ever come to Seattle and stay with us?"

"Too far. . . too much money," I joked.

Punching me hard and fast in the shoulder, she said, "Cheapskate. You have money!"

"Yeah—but. . ."

"But nothing. Where's your priorities?"

"Mm—I'll think on that. So where do we go?"

With a look of hesitation, Jennifer said, "I'm not sure." Turning her head toward me, she beckoned. "Shall we go in?"

"Let's go." I walked alongside her to the doors. As we neared them, I quickly grabbed the right one and held it open for her. "I'd say ladies first, but you're no lady!" I laughed.

Wordlessly, Jennifer pursed her lips and stomped on my foot as she walked by.

When we stepped inside, there was a short hallway that turned to the left and opened into a big room with red carpet. There were casket displays discreetly placed around the room, each with different finishes, shades of color, and increasing price tags to match.

"Can I help you?" a plump, older woman asked in barely audible voice.

I thought to myself, *Why are we whispering? Will the dead hear us?* "Yes—hi, I'm James, and this is my sister Jennifer."

Shaking each of our hands with soft, delicate hands, she whispered, "It's nice to meet you. What can I do for you?"

Jennifer interjected, "We need to make arrangements to

transfer our dad from the coroner's office and have his body cremated."

"Nothing complicated. We just need to fill out some forms to transfer the body to us, and we'll send you with paperwork so you can take his ashes."

"Perfect," Jennifer said with a satisfied voice.

Jennifer and I made all of the arrangements with the funeral home. They could have his ashes ready in three days. As we didn't know when the memorial would be or what church we could use, we agreed. Likely, we wouldn't be ready in three days anyway.

When we reached the cars, I turned to Jennifer and said, "Hey, I was thinking we should all go to Universal Studios while we are here. They have this attraction called Mel's Diner that is set up like a 1950s drive-in with old cars. I think Dad would love it if we did something fun like that."

Nodding her head in agreement, Jennifer said, "I think that's a great idea."

"Should we head over to our hotel and see what Sophia found out?"

"Yes—let's do it. I'll follow you."

"What, you like being lost?" I joked. "Can that turd even keep up?"

She laughed. "Nope. Drive nice and slow for me."

We got into our cars and caravanned along the streets of Orlando until we found my hotel.

CHAPTER TWENTY-TWO

Sophia contacted Our Lady of Lourdes and spoke with the priest who was sympathetic to our situation. He scheduled a memorial mass in five days. We just had to make a donation to the music director and another donation to the women who organized the post–funeral reception, serving a light lunch.

I called Uncle David and Aunt Patti, informing them of the memorial mass date and time. Jennifer called our mom and shared all the details with her. Mom and Jack would make plans to fly out with Tommy. With the memorial being held in Orlando, we didn't expect any others to come. Once everything was set in motion, I kicked myself for not driving home with the ashes and planning a memorial in Denver. I just wasn't thinking. I suppose a murder and waiting around for ashes in a strange city will do that to you.

The week was momentarily brightened when we all went to Universal Studios. The kids seemed enthralled by all of the sights and likely all the junk food they got to eat. Jennifer and I reminisced about Dad and the crazy times we had. I had completely forgotten about the weekend he took us camping and let Jennifer drink a California Cooler and I shot bottle rockets out of the truck's window while we drove down the road, Tommy wedged in between Jennifer and I.

On the day of the memorial, we arrived at the church. Dressed in a suit, I walked alongside Sophia, who wore an emerald–green dress and high heels that clacked against the cement. We remained somber and silent as we approached the church.

When we entered the church, we were greeted with mixed smells of incense and burning votive candles. Everything was quiet. As we walked farther into the vestibule across the thick, spongy red carpet, I noticed the picture collage Jennifer had made. It was propped on a wooden easel and contained many old pictures of our dad.

My mom and Jack quietly walked over to us looking glum. I smiled inwardly as her appearance was a familiar sight, with shoulder–length curled blonde hair, blue eyes, and wearing a red dress and white pearls. Jack was dressed in a freshly minted suit. A staple of his appearance was the neatly trimmed law enforcement mustache.

As they approached, my mom extended her arms and hugged me tightly. With her head next to mine, she whispered, "How are you doing?"

In a shaky voice, I replied, "Okay, I guess. Everything really hit me as we were walking into the church." Sniffling, I backed away from my mom, who briefly gazed into my eyes with a look of sympathy. Jack silently leaned in for a hug, patting my back. "Where's Tommy? I thought he was coming."

With a look of disappointment, Mom replied, "He had

a relapse. The stress was just too much for him." Turning her gaze to Sophia, Mom said, "Sophia, you look lovely as usual." She leaned forward and hugged Sophia tightly. As they separated, Mom asked, "How are the wedding plans coming?"

In a hushed tone, Sophia replied, "They are moving along. We need to make a trip to Breckenridge in the fall so we can line up a caterer, flowers, and everything else."

"Where's Jennifer?" I asked.

Mom turned her head from side to side. "Uh—she's around here somewhere."

Turning to walk away, I said, "I think I'll go find her before we sit down."

The memorial service started a while later. The memorial service was just like any other mass except for pews full of parishioners worshipping. When the priest finished his homily, he invited us to say a few words about Dad.

Shaking within, I slowly approached the podium, dabbing my eyes and wiping snot on my balled-up handkerchief. Taking a piece of paper from a pocket inside my jacket, I unfolded it and smoothed it on the podium, sounds of crumbling paper echoing through the microphone. All eyes were focused on me as I read, "We are here today asking Jesus to come and lead my dad to his new dwelling. As his life was special and unique, so too is the place Jesus prepared for him. We are confident in this because of Jesus' merciful love. He was always there to lend a hand when someone needed it. He would share feelings and life with those close to him and even strangers who didn't know him." I nervously chuckled. Continuing, I read,

"He was a person who was liked by anyone who had the good fortune to meet him. He brought a lot of laughter and good times to all of us. This is what it's all about and what Jesus taught us. As we heard in the Book of Wisdom today, 'Grace and mercy are with his holy ones, and his care is with his elect.' Throughout all of his struggles and tribulations within himself, he always glimmered amongst the stars of God's elect. My dad's life serves as a reminder to us that we should keep a watchful eye on those special stars." I briefly paused. "The ones that teach us something about life. I know this, because as both my friend and father, he left with me a way to live life and seek truth. He was an incredibly forgiving and remorseful man, and God knows this. You should know it too. As his soul lives on in heaven, so too does his memory in our hearts." Breaking down, I wept as I walked back to my pew. As I sat down, Sophia squeezed my hand in hers.

The rest of the day was a blur. I felt spent of all energy as we ate together during the reception. I briefly spoke with Uncle David and Aunt Patti. We hadn't spoken in a few years and our conversation was clunky and awkward. Afterwards, we said our goodbyes and drove back to our respective hotels.

When Sophia and I reached our hotel, I turned to her. "Before the funeral I talked to Jennifer—I decided to take my dad home with me. He doesn't belong here. He belongs in Colorado with us."

Sophia smiled. "James, I think that is a wonderful idea. Are you going to bury him or keep his ashes with you?"

"I want to bury him at Fort Logan National Cemetery. I remember him saying he wanted to be buried there someday."

"Then you should do it."

Sophia and I sat close to each other in the hotel gardens holding hands for a while. As the day's events wore on me, I told her I needed a nap and went into my hotel room. When I got up later that afternoon, we ate dinner in the rooftop restaurant.

CHAPTER TWENTY-THREE

Sophia and I were the last to leave Orlando; she flew home, and I drove to Denver with my dad's ashes in my car. I felt like he was with me while I drove the car listening to classic road trip bands like the Eagles, Jimmy Buffet, Lynyrd Skynyrd, Bob Seger, and the Beach Boys. Sometimes I imagined conversations with my dad and other times I sang along with the songs.

Once I located a copy of his DD-14, I arranged a memorial service and burial at Fort Logan National Cemetery. Unlike the mass in Orlando, the service at the cemetery had a large gathering. I was happy so many people came out to honor him. The gun salute's shots rang out, and tears filled our eyes. It was a closing out of a bygone era, one filled with dad's crazy capers. He was in peace.

Sophia and I continued with wedding plans.

With the trunk lid of my Mustang open, I walked into the house to grab the rest of my stuff. I could hear the engine slightly revving as it warmed. The carport was filled with light from the noonday sun. Sophia was driving up to Breckenridge as soon as she was out of an afternoon meeting.

Fall had begun. The trees around my house had begun the yearly festival, proudly displaying shades of red, yellow, and orange like a fourth of July fireworks show. The weather was still warm, and lawns throughout the neighborhood lay before homes like green carpets. Smatterings of red and yellow leaves rested against the green grass.

The weather girl on 9 News forecasted a possible winter storm in the high country. I was nervous about driving the Mustang to Breckenridge.

I turned north on Colorado Boulevard, heading toward I-70. The Mustang quickly climbed to fifty miles per hour before I eased up on the gas pedal. As I reached the stop light at 40th Avenue, I lifted my foot off the gas and slightly braked before I began to head down the steep hill. I turned on my signal and moved into the left lane.

When I reached the Pinewood Plaza shopping center at the bottom of the hill, a white SUV came flying out of the parking lot, swerving in front of me. Instinctively reacting, I stomped my right foot on the brake pedal. As the front and rear brakes of my Mustang clamped down, the rear end spun to the left side as I jerked the steering wheel right. While I skidded toward the SUV, tires screeching, the SUV continued in an arcing path in front of me. Rather than stopping, the driver seemed to go faster. With my car in a sideways skid, I looked out the driver's side window and saw the white SUV quickly approaching me. When I was a few feet away, the SUV crossed the left lane, turning wildly into the middle lane. Barely missing the SUV, I continued braking and then lifted my foot off the brake so that I could steer back left and straighten the car. As I did that, my Mustang violently fishtailed and I nearly slammed into the center median. Subconsciously my foot hit the brake pedal again. Luckily my car skidded straight, and I rapidly slowed down as I approached the stop light at Colorado Boulevard and 45th Avenue. My heart was pounding so hard my head throbbed. I had a feeling of terror and lightheadedness. My hands shook uncontrollably on the steering wheel while I continued down Colorado Boulevard. I wondered if I should just go home. Shaking and feeling dizzy, I continued through the stoplight at 45th Avenue, driving toward I-70. As I drove, many of the lights that I normally stopped at remained green.

When I reached I-70, the light turned red and I stopped in the left turn lane under the bridge. Breathing heavily, I mentally tried to calm myself down. I burst into a fit of screaming, hurling every swear word in my vocabulary at the windshield. I must have been yelling loudly because a guy sitting in his BMW on my right side turned and looked at me. Realizing I probably seemed like a lunatic, I quit yelling and stared forward. When the light turned green, I quickly accelerated onto the ramp. Accelerating rapidly, I merged onto I-70 and continued west toward Breckenridge.

As I looked out the windshield, I could see the mountains to the west. The sun was shining brightly, and everything seemed vivid in color. The iridescent mountains looked Persian blue, unwaveringly standing against the azure sky. The grass alongside the road looked sun burnt and devoid of life. It was late fall, and the trees were a mix of green, yellow, and red. As I looked at the trees, I wondered about the weather in the mountains. It can be sunny in Denver and blizzarding in the mountains on any given day. Colorado is renowned for its erratic weather. As I took in the sights along I-70 I decided to switch on some road trip music.

As "Take It Easy" came on, I turned the volume up just before the lyrics, "Well, I'm a-runnin' down the road tryin' to loosen my load" started. I smiled inwardly and continued driving west.

The chunk of highway between Denver and Breckenridge was tedious in places and in other places delightfully picturesque. In Idaho Springs I was dazzled by Clear Creek's white capped, steel blue water snaking through the mountains, occasionally revealing shiny, dark grey rocks with logs jammed around them like floating toothpicks.

Snowflakes began to fall like shimmering diamonds, and the highway became slicked with ice. *The drive is going to get rough*, I thought. Upon entering the Eisenhower Tunnel, I hoped a storm wasn't raging on the other side.

CHAPTER TWENTY-FOUR

The inside of the cabin was dark, except for the orange–yellow firelight that flickered, licking the walls and casting a dim yellow light on the planked wood floor and log furniture. I could feel a searing heat pulsing from the fireplace, which was bordered with simple gray bricks and a shallow mantel. There was a round, faded green, rustic hearth rug between my chair and the fireplace. The room smelled like cooked garlic and cumin. I was wrapped in a heavy, quilted blanket, though my body was chilled. As I turned my head, I saw darkness beyond the firelight. It seemed ominous and mysterious. My head was pounding.

A few feet away was an older man sitting in a log chair, gazing in my direction. He appeared to be sixty or seventy years old with curly white hair and hazel eyes. His face was rounded with prominent lips. He was slender and dressed in a black–and–red checkered flannel shirt with faded blue jeans. He seemed fairly tall, though I couldn't be sure. "My name is Michael Morris." he said with a deep voice.

I felt disoriented and confused. The stranger's voice seemed far away—like I was inside a glass box and he was yelling from outside of it. I struggled to find my voice, "James Fisher. Um, what did you say your name was?"

"Michael Morris."

"How did I get here?"

"I found you wandering in the cold. There's a big bump on your head, so I figured you hit your head somewhere."

Reaching my hand up, I felt a massive bump on the right side of my head. I flinched as the sharp pain jarred me. Michael's voice seemed strangely familiar to me, yet I didn't know why. "I don't remember hitting my head—I don't even remember how I got here," I said.

Nodding, Michael said, "When I found you wandering in the snow, I helped you into my truck and drove you back to my cabin. You were mumbling something about the disease stopping with you. When we arrived at the cabin, I laid you down on the couch and wrapped you in the quilted blanket. Your boots were soaked all the way through, so I took them off and put them over by the door. You've been fading in and out for a couple hours."

"I must have blacked out. I feel like my brain is being squeezed in a bench vise, and everything feels heavy."

Rising to his feet, Michael said, "Let me see if I have some Advil."

Struggling to sit up on the couch, I said, "That would help a lot."

Michael walked into the darkness and disappeared. I noticed he was wearing heavy boots that produced a knocking sound against the wood floor. I saw a light turn on in the back room and heard things moving around, like someone was rummaging through a box of derelict items. After a few seconds, the sounds stopped, and the light was extinguished. I saw Michael walk back into the flickering light from the darkness, as if he appeared from nowhere. He extended his hand toward me and said, "Here you go. Let me get you a glass of water."

Reaching my hand out of the blanket, I took the Advil from him and said, "Thank you."

Michael turned and walked back into the darkness. I heard a cabinet creak open and then the sound of water running. Again, Michael seemed to appear out of the darkness. He extended his arm toward me with a glass in his hand.

I reached up and grabbed the glass of water. "Ah, Thank you."

After handing the water to me, Michael walked back to the log chair and sat down. "I have some chili in the crockpot. We can eat some dinner when you feel up to it."

I put the two Advil caplets into my mouth and took a sip of water. It was cold and sent a chill throughout my body. Trying to regain warmth, I tugged the blanket closer to my body with my free hand. "Where is this cabin at? I mean, where am I?" I asked.

"We are about twelve miles southeast of Breckenridge on route 850. Highway 9 is the only way out of this area." Looking over toward the door, he added, "Nothing but forest between here and Breckenridge."

"I was headed to Breckenridge. My fiancée and I were planning to stay for a couple of days while we coordinated some of the wedding details," I said.

"I figured you were headed somewhere in this area. I found you down by Highway 9. I was on my way home from the grocery store in Breckenridge and saw you stumbling along a ditch," Michael said. He smoothed his white hair back and sighed before he spoke again. "Man, you were in bad shape! Any idea what happened?"

"I don't remember, but thanks for picking me up. As I cold as I am, I was probably close to freezing to death."

Smiling, he replied, "It's no trouble, though getting you inside was a bit tricky. It was snowing pretty hard—I could barely see where the road was. As I drove up here, I had to stop and put chains on my truck. When I finally reached the cabin, there was about eight inches on the ground. I had to practically drag you inside." Laughing he joked, "Either my arms have gotten weak, or you are heavy."

With a brush of amusement, I countered, "Perhaps I snacked on too many donuts on the way up." Shuddering under the blanket and drawing the blanket tighter, I asked in a bashful voice, "Do you have anything hot? Maybe some tea? I just can't seem to warm up."

"I sure do, bud," Michael said, as he slowly got up from the chair. He walked over to me and took the glass of water from my hand. Then he turned and walked into the darkness. As he disappeared, I wrapped both of my arms under the blanket and curled my feet closer to my body. This time a faint yellow light above the kitchen sink switched on. Craning my head sideways, I could see Michael grabbing a tea kettle off the stove and walking over to the sink. In the dim light, the kitchen looked old, like something from the 1940s. The cabinets were light oak colored with long rounded chrome pulls. Chrome edging ran along the low kitchen counter. I heard Michael turn the kitchen faucet on and fill the tea kettle. When the tea kettle was full of water, Michael turned sideways and stepped over to the stove. With the tea kettle setting on the stove, he reached toward the dial to switch the heat on. Leaving the kitchen light on, Michael walked back to his chair. "It may take a few minutes for the water to boil," he said.

"Thank you. I hope I'm not causing you any trouble. I can go to a hotel if you want," I said sheepishly.

Chortling, he replied, "Don't worry about it, bud. The snow is way too deep now. Even with chains on the truck, it would be hell driving down the road. Besides, I have this nice log chair to sit on. I don't need the couch."

With an exaggerated sigh, I said, "Are you sure? Just let me know when I've overstayed my welcome." Bud? It was weird to hear him call me that. My dad always called me bud.

"Nope, it's already settled. The couch is yours, and that's final," he said, in a deep voice.

Giving up, I said, "Well, thanks. When the storm lets up, I'll get out of your way."

Michael seemed like an easy–going guy. I couldn't believe he picked me up on the side of the road and brought me up here. The cabin seemed peaceful and cozy. For some odd reason I had a sense of peace with Michael.

"While we wait for the water to boil, why don't you tell me about yourself," Michael said. Reaching for a coke on the end table, he said, "Where are you from?"

"Well, my *life* would be a very long story."

"We've got all night, James. Likely that storm won't let up until tomorrow sometime."

Normally I would be guarded and suspicious of a stranger, and certainly with one who asks to hear my life story in a secluded cabin. Oddly with Michael I didn't feel that way. There was a comfortable familiarity about him.

Grinning, I said, "We may need to switch to coffee. Well, I was born in California. My dad was in the navy when I was little, and we lived in San Francisco and San

Diego. When he got out of the service, we moved to Colorado. Both of my parents were from small towns in northeastern Colorado, so we moved near family. During my elementary school years, we lived in Denver. A few weeks before I started high school, we moved to Sierra Vista, which is a small town in the southwest corner of Arizona. I started college in Arizona but didn't stay. My parents split up my first semester of college. When my mom moved back to Denver, I went with her. I had to wait until I was a resident of Colorado to get back into college, so I just worked and saved money for a year. I graduated from the UCD and have stayed in Denver ever since. When I was in college, I started working for a good company and eventually established an IT career. After college, I rediscovered a woman who is my soon to be wife, and here we are."

Suddenly, the kettle in the kitchen began to whistle loudly. Rising to his feet, Michael chuckled and said, "Sounds like the abridged version." Then he turned and walked over to the kitchen. "I'll be right back—then I want to hear the long version."

"But it's our first date," I said, jokingly. Turning my head upward, I raised my voice. "I want to hear your story."

Michael opened the upper cupboard next to the sink, grabbed a mug and filled it with hot water from the tea kettle. Then he grabbed a tea bag from a box on the counter and dunked into the mug. After switching off the light above the sink, he walked through the darkness and handed the hot mug to me. Watching the steam rise off the top, I slowly wrapped my fingers around the handle and brought it down to my chest, holding on to it through the quilt.

Ignoring what I said, Michael resumed his questioning. "I lived in Denver for years. What side of town did you live on?"

"Mostly southwest—we moved around every couple of years. I went to four different schools during my elementary and junior high years."

"Was that hard? Changing schools all the time?

Hesitating for a moment, I answered, "Um, a little bit. I guess I never really got that close to any friends, and school always felt like a movie—something I watched rather than being a part of. Sometimes I wonder what life would have been like if I had stayed in one place—and had close friends."

I raised the mug to my lips, squinting as I cautiously took a sip of tea. My tongued singed a little, but it felt good to have the mug near my face.

Briefly ruminating with my gaze upward, I continued, "Changing schools was tough, I suppose. But I also have good memories of moving to new places and exploring the neighborhoods on my bike. I used to love riding around checking stuff out. Funny, every place we lived had an exciting feature. Near one house, there was a place called the bike hills at the end of the neighborhood. I used to spend my Saturdays riding my bike up and down these huge dirt hills. There was a big ditch lined with massive trees. In the summer I would pick up my bike and wade through the water to the other side. In the fall and winter when it was dry, I would ride down one side of the ditch and up the other. The bike hills were a blast. At another place in southwest Denver, we lived near the Platte River. I used to ride the trails along the river, exploring for miles. The first time I ever saw a homeless person under a bridge was while I was riding along the river." After pausing briefly, I continued, "Sorry, I didn't mean to carry on about where I rode my bike."

I took a drink of my tea which had cooled to a comfortable level. As the warm water entered my body, it warmed me. I started to feel more energized as I warmed up.

Michael had a bright smile on his face. His hazel eyes twinkled. "It sounds like you had a lot of fun. Life was kind of bittersweet."

Looking upwards, I thoughtfully replied, "I suppose."

"Sierra Vista. What was that town like?" Michael asked.

"I'll get to that. I've been talking for a while, and I want to hear about you—where are you from?" I said. Taking a drink of tea, I raised my eyebrows, smiling while I made a shooing gesture with my free hand. "Go on."

CHAPTER TWENTY-FIVE

After adjusting himself in his chair, Michael began, "Bud, my story is like yours. I moved around a lot. I was born in Denver, but at the time my parents lived in Sagebrush, Colorado. My dad was restless and moved us around quite a bit. When I was in third grade, my dad sold our house in Sagebrush and moved us to Denver. We lived in southeast Denver for a couple years and then moved to Los Angeles, California. We lived there for a couple years until my dad decided he wanted to go back to Colorado. He bought our house in Sagebrush back from the guy he sold it to, and we moved in. I went to Sagebrush High School until I joined the navy and left home. I joined the navy during the Viet Nam war, so I spent some time in the Gulf of Tonkin, assigned to an amphibious transport ship. Our ship also sailed to Hong Kong, the Philippines, Hawaii, and Japan. In fact, I served on one of the first ships to port in Japan after World War II. In the late seventies I got out of the navy and moved back to Colorado. I lived in

Fort Meyers for a while and then moved to Denver. I mostly drove a truck and worked in autobody shops."

"I haven't been to Sagebrush. What is that like?" I asked.

"Sagebrush is like most of northeastern Colorado—flat with sunflowers and tumbleweeds. We lived about fifteen miles south of town off Highway 71. The country roads are part paved and part dirt. The main industries are farming, cattle ranching, and dairies."

"It sounds like a boring place. Did you like living there?"

"Like you, I found things to do. I had a horse that I took care of and rode along the dirt roads. There were oil drills nearby our house that I used to climb up on and ride up and down while they pumped oil. I kept myself occupied. We always end up where we are supposed to. I'll tell you an interesting pattern. My dad was in the first graduating class of Sagebrush High School, and I was in the last. After I graduated, they tore the building down and moved into a new building."

Michael's comments piqued my interest. "I was in the first graduating class at my high school in Sierra Vista. I also had a weird pattern like that. My dad graduated from high school in 1971 and I graduated from high school in 1991. I wouldn't have even graduated in 1991 if I hadn't been held back a year. Funny you mentioned patterns. I've always noticed strange patterns in my life like that."

"Life is full of patterns. If we look closely, our lives are a narrative in a story that intersects in strange but purposeful ways."

Nodding my head in agreement, I drank the remaining tea and set the mug down on the table next to my chair.

Continuing, Michael said, "I recently moved into this

secluded cabin, and I have a lot of time to reflect on my life now. A lot of people are afraid of acknowledging God—acknowledging there is something greater than our human existence. Looking at how my life unfolded, I've realized that the patterns or intersections of our life are signs that life is progressing as it should be. Nothing is random." After speaking, he paused, letting his words hang in the air. "James, we'll talk more about my life, but tell me more about Sierra Vista."

This conversation was getting deep—sort of philosophical. How did we go from simple small talk to the existence of God and the meaning of life? Ugh. The poor old guy must not get many opportunities for conversation. He probably saved my life, so I figured I'd humor him.

"I'm not sure if you have been to Sierra Vista—"

"I haven't. Where's it at?" Michael interjected.

"Sierra Vista is a small town in the southwest corner of Arizona, right next to the California and Mexico border. The Colorado River intersects with the town on its way to Mexico. The town is mostly famous for the territorial prison. Back in the late 1800s it was basically Alcatraz of the desert."

"Hmm. The area sounds familiar. I probably blew past it on weekend trips back to Colorado when I was stationed in San Diego."

His comment made me laugh. "Yes—I suppose you would have blown past it. It sits a ways off of Highway 8. Though I'm curious—how did you drive to Colorado on a weekend? That's like a thousand miles."

"I was young, bud," Michael said, with a wide grin on his face. "I had a hell of a lot more energy than I have now."

"You must've," I said with amazement. "When I was in college, I used to drive back to see my friends—but not over a weekend. You must have been a badass!" Chuckling, I adjusted myself on the couch.

"I was. Now tell me about this hidden town." He raised his eyebrows. "What did I miss?"

"You are curious, aren't you? In relation to the desert southwest, Sierra Vista was like an oasis. Not sure if you remember the area, but southwest Arizona is mostly sand, volcanic rock, and chocolaty looking mountain ranges. If the government wanted to fake a planetary landing, that area would be perfect. The area around Sierra Vista looks nothing like the areas around Phoenix and Tucson where you see thousands of saguaros, organ pipe, or cholla cactuses. It's dead looking. Conversely, Sierra Vista is a fairly green town. Because of the dams on the Colorado River, farm crops surround the town and many of the houses have green lawns. Along with palm trees, there are all kinds of trees imported from California and Mexico. Many of the homes have swimming pools and the streets were clean. It's small—maybe 150,000 people yet feels larger because it's spread out. There are three high—"

"Wait," Michael interjected. "Tell me more about your life in Sierra Vista."

His words jolted me. I suppose I was rambling. "What do you mean?" I inquired.

"Tell me about your move there—schools, girlfriends, your first car. . ." Michael waved his hand in a circular motion, suggesting more things.

"Ah. Okay, well, we moved to Sierra Vista the week I was supposed to start high school in Denver. This was a blessing because I would have gone to one of the roughest high schools in the city. I remember we stayed a few days at my uncle's house before finding a home." I began to laugh. "I remember when my uncle drove me, my mom, and my sister to each of Sierra Vista's two high schools. First, he drove us to Desert Hills High School. It seemed nice. The buildings were spread out with white V–style roofs. There was a large park surrounding it with rolling hill covered in grass and palm trees. It looked more like a school in California than Arizona. Then he drove us across town to Valley Union High School. It wasn't as nice looking as Desert Hills. In fact, it looked worn out and old. But then, I saw a group of hot–looking blonde chicks walk out. Right away, I was like, that's the school. I want to go to this one!" I said, starting to laugh uncontrollably.

Michael was smiling wide, and his eyes were round and bright. "Hey, I'd do the same. You've gotta go where the cute girls are. Did anyone realize you picked the school because you saw some pretty blondes?"

"I'm not sure. No one said anything if they did. But thinking about it now, I wonder if they did," I said, beginning to reflect on that day.

"So, life must've been grand at harem high," Michael said jokingly.

"I guess—I was a dorky freshman and didn't go out with any of the blondes, if that's what you mean. Ironically, the two girls I liked weren't blondes at all. One was a brunette and the other was a redhead." I shook my head, feigning shame. "It's crazy to look back on it. I chased the brunette from my Algebra class all year. I even remember a stupid line she told me. 'I think we should stay friends because anything else would ruin things.' What crap! Girls —why can't they just say they aren't interested?"

Michael shrugged his shoulders and moved his head side to side. "Women!"

"The redhead was always a mystery or was at the time, anyway. We had art class together, and I was infatuated with her artsy personality and the way she dressed. But she always seemed distant and walled off. At the time I thought she was weird or wasn't interested in me. Later, I found out that her dad was a total pervert and was molesting her. No wonder she always kept her distance. Figures though. I've always been attracted to people who are screwed up." Chuckling, I shook my head. "Anyway, I wasn't quite the ladies' man I had hoped to be."

"When you weren't chasing girls, what did you do?"

"My freshman year was a strange year. The first week of school I met two friends. One was this blond surfer–looking dude who was a total chick magnet. The other was more of a nerd who took AP classes. They were very different from each other, but that's how I was. I never moved in cliques or groups. I sort of gravitated toward people I could trust. Other than when I saw those two in class or after school, I really didn't have any friends. I remember lunch hour being awkward. I didn't have anyone to hang out with, and I certainly didn't want anyone real-izing that I had no one to hang out with. So I wandered around trying to look busy during lunch—this part will make you laugh. Again, trying to look busy, I frequently went to the counselor's office, asking about classes and stuff. Sometimes I would even sit in long lines waiting to get into the counselor's office. Well, that of course back-fired on me and the counselor put me in group therapy because he thought I was crazy." I began to laugh uncon-trollably. After I stopped laughing, I continued, "I can't hardly blame them—who goes to the counselor's office on their own? Anyway, like I said, it was a weird year. I think I was more lost than anything. All throughout my child-hood, I had always had focus or was busy with something. I played all kinds of sports—soccer, baseball, volleyball, and basketball. When I wasn't in sports, I was pursuing academic clubs such as decathlon or MESA—uh, Math Engineering Science Association. So not really having something threw me off. But. . . I was a fortunate kid in many ways. My uncle who owned a full–service laundromat gave me a job." Looking upwards while I chuckled, I said, "Of course he had to test the waters at first—have me prove that I was a good worker. First, I had to scrub all of the laundry carts with soap and water. Well, I didn't just clean them; I made them look brand new. Though, I can't take all of the credit. My dad stopped by one day and said, 'If you're gonna do it, do it right.' He found a can of WD-40 and suggested I oil the wheels while I'm at it." When I looked over, I saw a twinkle–eyed smile on Michael's face. "Once the carts were cleaned, he tasked me with cleaning the lint boxes behind the dryers. This was a horrible job, but exciting at the same time. I had to work at night when the laundromat was closed, and it involved squeezing myself behind the dryers with a screwdriver and unhooking the vent hoses so I could clean out the boxes in the ceiling. When I completed that, he gave me a job as an attendant. From the beginning of my freshman year until I moved away from Sierra Vista, I worked in the laundromat. At the time, I didn't particularly like sweating in a hot laundromat all the time, or having to wash people's nasty clothes, but looking back that job taught me a lot about responsibility and managing myself. Because of that job, I ended up far more mature than other kids when I was in college."

"I imagine so, bud." Michael leaned back and rubbed his belly. "Man, I'm starving. How do you feel, James? Do you want some chili?"

"I'm feeling much better. The Advil finally kicked in

and my head isn't hurting as bad as it was. Yeah, I could go for some chili."

"It settled. Let's eat." Michael stood up and walked toward the kitchen.

After setting the empty mug on the end table, I threw off the blanket and put my feet down on the cold floor. As I stood up, I became dizzy for a moment, like my blood sugar was low. Once the dizziness subsided, I started to walk around the couch and head toward the kitchen.

When Michael arrived in the kitchen, he opened a cupboard and grabbed two bowls while asking, "Do you like cheese and sour cream?" Not waiting for a reply, he set the bowls down on the counter near the crockpot and reached into the refrigerator, producing a bag of shredded cheese and sour cream. "Help yourself."

"It sure smells good." I said, smiling. I had that familiar sense of warmth, bundled up on a warm house on a cold, snowy evening.

After Michael and I ladled chili into our bowls and added cheese and sour cream, we sat down at a small, circular dining table that had four chairs. There were red placements at each sitting position. Michael and I sat opposite each other.

Breaking the silence, Michael said, "Let's say grace."

As I bowed my head, Michael led us in prayer. "Bless us, o Lord, and these Thy gifts, which we are about to receive from Thy bounty. Through Christ, our Lord, Amen." When he finished, we both gestured the sign of the cross and raised our heads. I picked up my spoon and began to stir the melting cheese into my chili. Then I spooned hot chili into my mouth, savoring the delicious blend of flavors of garlic, cumin, and chili powder. I felt strangely comforted by the warm chili.

Michael lifted a spoon of chili to his mouth. After he swallowed it, he said, "I hope you like it. I think I added a bit too much garlic."

"No, it's really good. And you picked a perfect night for it." I said, smiling.

"Sounds like your freshman year of high school was pretty good—aside from the counselor who thought you were crazy." Michael winked at me.

I laughed. "Yeah, for the most part—we moved to Sierra Vista so that my dad could get a fresh start, away from the city where he had a lot of drug connections and bad influences. The first few months were good, but later he found the same types of friends again."

"Wait, back up. You moved to Sierra Vista so that your dad could get away from drug users?"

Chuckling, I said, "Well, I guess that needs some explanation. Basically, throughout my childhood and preteen years, he partied all the time, drinking and using cocaine. A number of times he would go out partying, and the next day his truck or car would be towed to the house, completely destroyed. In fact, I have no idea how he survived rolling his truck several times in one accident. He must have had an incredible guardian angel. He frequently disappeared for days or skipped holidays and birthdays to get drunk, partying with friends. Anyway, things got really bad and my mom finally kicked him out. As a second chance, we moved to Sierra Vista."

"It sounds like you had a crazy childhood."

"I did. But as I said before, I always found the brighter side of things. I never grew up hating him or anything. I wasn't one of those bitter kids who pouted about their life. That's all I knew. You know what I mean?"

Shrugging, Michael said, "Yeah."

"Anyway, back to what I was saying, my freshman year was weird. It was kind of a transitional year. The highlight of it was when I got my driving permit toward the end of the school year. Starting at eleven or twelve, I began fantasizing about driving, thinking about Chevelles, Corvettes, Barracudas, Mustangs—anything with a loud motor and fat tires. So driving was huge for me. I saved just about every penny I made at the laundromat so I could buy my first car. For months, my dad and I went out cruising on Saturday mornings. Honestly, I think he enjoyed it as much as I did. He would always pour a thermos of coffee and drink it while he directed me around town. More often than not, we would head out to the country and sight-see." When I stopped talking, I noticed Michael was smiling at me. He seemed happy."

"I'm sure he loved riding around in the car with you." He spooned some chili in his mouth, looking thoughtful. "What was the next year like?"

"Wait, I want to hear about you. I feel like I'm telling my life story to a shrink," I chided.

"Fair enough, bud. As I said earlier, we moved quite a bit. At the end of my eight–grade year, my dad decided he wanted to move back to Sagebrush." He began to laugh. "I remember when we arrived in town. My older brother and I were wearing black sunglasses, plaid Bermuda shorts, and white button–up shirts, standing on the street corner of downtown Sagebrush. People were walking by, staring at us like we'd arrived from outer space. Folks in northeastern Colorado weren't used to seeing Californians." He laughed heartily. "We were quite the spectacle. Even though I had lived there for a while when I was a younger, it was like starting over in a new place. Moving to Sagebrush from Los Angeles was a hard adjustment. Like you, I had to start over with friends. Unfortunately, I fell in with the wrong kids who drank and ditched school. For me, that was the beginning of a life of bad choices. My dad used to let me drive the tractor around the house and drive his pickup on the country roads. A permit wasn't as monumental as it was for other kids. Now, my first car, that was monumental. When I turned sixteen, my parents bought me a 1964 Ford Falcon. The car was only four years old, so it felt new. The Falcon had a 260, which was the popular small–block motor before they started making 289s."

"Cool. My first car was a '79 Mustang. I guess we're both Ford guys." I said, approvingly.

"Yeah, sounds like it."

After swallowing the last bite of chili, I nodded my head and pursed my lips. Feeling satisfied, I said, "Thank you. That hit the spot."

"You're welcome," Michael said, bigheartedly. In a prodding gesture, he lifted his hand up, open palmed. "On to your sophomore year. What was that like?"

"This may come as a shocker, but I changed schools. I just got settled in at Valley Union High School, and as my luck would have it, they built a new high school and I fell into its zone. So, I started my sophomore year at Sierra Vista. My nerdy friend Rick changed schools with me, but I didn't have any classes with him. In fact, even though he and I stayed friends and did stuff outside of school, I never had a class with him. Anyway, I started over in many ways, though that year was a bit easier because I joined the swim team. From that year on, the kids I was on the swim team with were like my tribe. I ate lunch with a bunch of them and hung out with a couple of the guys after school. When I look back, they all had their own cliques and groups, but I just floated outside of them, hanging out with friends individually. In the fall, I got my license and bought my first car. Um, you already know that it was a '79 Mustang. It was originally some old lady's car, and then her son inherited it when she died. He kind of trashed it. The silver paint was completely sun faded and oxidized; the tires were nearly bald, and it had about eighty-thousand miles on it. Needless to say, it needed some TLC. Most of my sophomore year was a blur. Once I got the car, my life sort of revolved around that. I had some money left over when I bought it, so I had it painted. My dad stripped the car completely down and we took it to a guy down in Mexico."

"Down in Mexico?" Michael said, inquisitively.

"Yes," I said with a chuckle. "Believe it or not, you could get a nice paint job down in Mexico for a fraction of what it cost in the US. For about three-hundred-fifty bucks, I had a sweet paint job."

"What color did you paint it?"

"It was this greenish–teal color with blue interior. I drove it for a couple of months until a head gasket blew. Luckily, my dad was a pretty good mechanic and took it apart for me. The car had to sit for a couple months until I saved up money to fix the heads. In early spring, I was happily driving again. Later that spring I needed tires. Of course, I didn't have the money, so I talked my grandfather into loaning me 800 bucks for some new wheels and fat tires. Like I said, that whole year was about my car," I said smiling. "I had dreamed of having a nice car since I was a kid—so I was determined to have a cool–looking car."

"That's it? Just the car?"

"Well, I owed by grandpa 800 bucks. He had no intention of letting me out of it. So yes, I was busy working for my car." I said jokingly. Reclaiming seriousness, I continued, "I remember swim trips. Rick and I started going to the tennis courts after school, and I got into playing tennis. My dad had his good moments and his bad. I vaguely remember some serious events. One time a drug dealer showed up at our house looking for his money. One time he broke into my grandparent's house, and they unexpectedly came home and found him shooting up with some weird dudes. But overall, I remember my car the most."

"Hmm. It sounds like your dad was caught between two worlds—being there for his family and addiction," Michael said while getting up. "Did you get enough? There's more chili in there."

"No—I'm good. Thank you."

"How about another cup of tea?"

"Sure. That would be good," I said gratefully.

Michael stood up, grabbed my empty bowl, and stacked it on top of his. Then he turned and walked over to the kitchen sink. While he rinsed the bowls, he spoke loudly over his shoulder, "What was your junior year like?"

"Are we going through my whole life?" I asked.

He turned around and faced me. "It may seem weird to go through our life stories when we could be talking cars, guns, or sports. But there's a point to this. You'll see." Michael said, curling half his mouth into a smile and winking. His look was knowing.

"Um, okay—this is weird, and I'm definitely not used to chronicling my life. In fact, I haven't thought about all of this in years."

Ignoring my protests, he grabbed the tea kettle and filled it with water. "Let's hear about your junior year." Turning around, he set the kettle down on a stove burner and turned the heat on.

I fixed my gaze away from the kitchen, looking into the darkest corner of the cabin. I could see orangish-yellow firelight moving on the walls. With each flicker of the light, dark shadows equally moved alongside. "Looking back, my junior year was transformational. The summer before my junior year, I met a blonde girl named Christine. It was love at first sight. We were on vacation, visiting family in Denver and my cousin took me to youth group at his church. When I walked to the front of the church, Christine turned and looked at me. She had translucent green eyes, and when she met my gaze, our eyes locked. I have no idea how long we stared at each other, but it seemed like time stopped and everything around us blurred—kind of like taking a selective focus picture using a telephoto lens and wide aperture. At first, we didn't speak. In fact, I didn't speak to her until we were crammed into a car together, riding to a youth group members house. I don't remember why we went there, but Christine had my full attention." I chuckled before continuing. "We talked through the evening and when it was time for me to go, we exchanged numbers and she kissed me on the cheek. While my cousin drove me back to the house, I was dazed and confused. Anyway, the beginning of the year was like the year before. I was on the swim team, I worked, and met up with friends to play tennis. Christine and I wrote letters back and forth and called each other every once in a while. Over the months, I began to yearn to be with my far away girlfriend. I—"

"I knew a few guys with girlfriends who lived out of town; some even had girls in Canada," Michael interrupted.

"Funny! Yes, but mine was real. The more I wanted to be with her, the more I changed within. I sort of became wilder, more brazen internally."

"Probably hormones."

"Yes, probably. It was more than that. Everything became more intense and in focus. When I heard a love song, it moved me more than it did when I was younger. Anyway, I saved up money and bought a plane ticket so I could go see her. I stayed with my aunt and my cousin drove me to see her a few times. That's when I transformed. I remember going to this hippy café place called Paris. It was a dark, swanky place where teens met up to drink highly caffeinated coffee and smoke. They even had poetry readings and full bookcases of literary classics. Christine dressed kind of punk and was artsy. Alongside her we moved among the artsy crowd, smoking clove cigarettes and sipping espresso. The coffee was nasty, but I quickly acquired a taste for cloves."

Shaking his head, Michael said, "I can't believe you smoked those—they're nasty."

"As I said, my eyes were opened to a whole new world. In fact, when I went home, I began dressing more punk, smoking clove cigarettes, sneaking out with my surfer friend to visit girls late at night. I was young and free. I stayed in this mode until the beginning of my senior year. And then a different change came, one that slowed me down."

"Back at that flagpole, chasing girls," Michael said, grinning while shaking his head. "Up until now you've shown that you are an achiever. You played sports, you joined clubs, you worked like a dog in order to have a nice car. Tell me it didn't stop there."

"No, I suppose not. Christine lived in another state. When I think about my junior year, my mind goes to romantic love letters and fantasies, not the day-to-day stuff. Like I said, my junior year was transformational, and not just hormonally. On the swim team, I stepped things up. In the second half of my sophomore year, I started getting serious about weightlifting. The summer before my junior year, I lifted weights five days a week, alternating upper body and legs. So, when swimming started, I was in far better shape than the other guys. I swam hard at practice and ultimately went to state. I continued to work hard at the laundromat. When the opportunity came up, I took a Maytag repair class in Phoenix so that I could work on washers and dryers. Thinking back, I can't believe my mom let me take a day off school for that. Anyway, I basically worked a second job at the laundromat repairing machines, making ten bucks an hour. That was big money back then. I began working hard to get good grades in school. Until my freshman year, I had maintained B averages. Some of my grades fell during freshman and sophomore year. But during my junior year, I started putting forth a lot more effort to bring my grades up."

"Now that is what I expected to hear. A struggle, a climb to something. That's what your whole life has been about!"

"Huh?" Michael's comment confused me. It was like he already knew my life story. A loud whistle erupted from the kitchen. Startled, I looked toward the kitchen. When I saw steam rising into the air, I realized it was the tea kettle.

"Time for tea," Michael said, as he stood up. Groaning, he slowly stood more upright, stretching his back. Stiffly, he walked toward the kitchen. When he reached the stove, he moved the kettle away from the hot burner and turned the stove off. Realizing he forgot to take our mugs into the kitchen, he turned and walked back to the dining table. "The mind isn't what it used to be." Grabbing a mug in each hand, he walked back into the kitchen and set the mugs down on the counter. He reached for the tea box and dropped a tea bag into each mug. He then grabbed the tea kettle and filled each mug with steaming hot water.

I watched Michael as he prepared our tea. He was a

strange man. What did he mean by *That's what your whole life has been about?* I could tell he was Christian. Maybe he was a preacher or ex-priest. There was a strange benevolence about him.

"Why don't we move over by the fireplace," Michael said as he walked toward the dining table. Stopping at the table, he handed my tea to me. Once I accepted the mug, he walked over to his chair and set his tea down on the end table.

Rising from my chair, I said, "Sure."

As I walked toward the couch with my tea, the yellow firelight danced upon my face, flickering wildly. I could feel the pulsing heat on my body.

Grabbing a log from the wooden box to the right of the fireplace, Michael said, "I think I'll add a couple of logs and stir the fire up."

When I reached the couch, I sat down, feeling relief from the soft cushions. The hard kitchen chair had made my butt sore.

Michael repositioned the burnt logs with a black metal poker and then set the new unburnt log on top. As he stirred the logs, the flames rose higher, wrapping themselves around the added log. I could hear crackles and pops as the bark began to ignite. The flames were mesmerizing and held my gaze. The blue flames at the bottom seemed to awaken my senses.

"Michael, what did you do in high school? Did you have a lot of girlfriends?" I said, breaking my gaze from the flames.

"James, in many ways I was aimless—more interested in goofing off with my friends," Michael said as he sat down.

"What do you mean?" I asked, sipping my tea. It tasted like vanilla.

Grabbing his tea from the end table, Michael replied, "My mom was musical and played piano. Because of her love for music, she pushed my sister and brother and I to choose an instrument. My oldest brother played piano, my sister played the clarinet, and I played the saxophone. During my freshman and sophomore year, I played in the high school band. During my freshman year, I was also in 4H. I never really enjoyed band or 4H, so I quit both of them my junior year. That was quite the scandal on the Morris farm! I remember my mother being angry that I quit band. Throughout my childhood I was often compared to my older brother, the golden child. He was an achiever, and I was not. I was the lost child in our family. He had good grades and played in band until he graduated and went to college. My grades were mediocre. I was capable of getting good grades, but I never applied myself. I was more interested in being social and goofing off with my friends." Michael sipped his tea, seeming to absorb the warmth from it. "Like you I was into hot rod cars. In fact, the muscle cars you dreamed of were brand new in my day. When I got my Falcon, I spent a lot of time figuring out how to soup it up." Michael laughed and let out a high–pitched sigh. "I used to unhook the exhaust pipes to make my engine louder and cruise Main Street. One time I unhooked the rear brakes so that I could do better burnouts!"

"Really?"

"Oh, yeah. I was like my dad, handy with stuff. I remember staying at my older brother's house in California my sophomore year. When he wasn't home, I took the exhaust pipes off his '66 Corvette and cruised around San Francisco, running straight headers."

"Awesome!"

"Excuse me. I need to hit the bathroom. Too much tea

and pop." Michael quickly got up from his chair and walked into the darkness. A light switched on in the bathroom, and he closed the door.

While Michael relieved himself, I ruminated on what he just told me. What a cool old guy. I wished I had lived when cars were cool like that. If I took the exhaust pipes off my Mustang, I'd likely get a ticket for over polluting the air. Man, times had changed. A minute later I saw a flash of light and then darkness. As the boot steps came closer, Michael appeared out of the darkness.

Sitting down in his chair and sighing in relief, Michael said, "Where was I?"

"Uh—you were talking about uncorking the headers on your brother's '66 Corvette. By the way, I'm jealous."

"Ah, yes—that was a fun day." Michael reached for his mug and took a sip of tea. "So what change slowed you down after your junior year?"

"Back to me already? You didn't tell me if you worked or not. Did you have rich parents or something?"

"I had a couple of jobs in high school. I worked as a bagger in a grocery store for a while. When I lost that job, I worked for my friend's dad in a hardware store. I worked off and on for gas money. My parents weren't the Rockefellers, but I did get an allowance for doing chores around the farm. One summer, my dad made me work on the fencing around our property, digging holes and replacing posts. I spent weeks driving the pickup around the property loaded with posts and barbwire rolls. If you want strong arms, work on a farm. I don't care how much weightlifting you do, a farm boy will kick your ass at arm wrestling." Michael winked at me. "Okay, bud, tell me about that slow down."

I drank some of my tea. This was a bittersweet story, and I didn't know how to begin. If the snow wasn't so bad,

I'd have Michael drive me to Breckenridge or wherever my car was. What the hell had happened to my car anyway? I couldn't even remember what happened. The conversation was becoming tedious. We just went back and forth talking about childhood. What was the point of this? Why was Michael so cryptic and quick to keep me talking? Sighing, I stared at the fire as if the flickering flames were a window into the past where I could transport myself. The dark red areas within the flames seemed to stir a sense of something ancient, something viscerally tied to my spirit.

"The beginning of my senior year was a continuation of my junior year. Over the summer I basically worked three jobs and saved up a bunch of money."

"Three jobs?"

"Yes," I said, with a grin. "I continued working at the laundromat as an attendant on the weekends and repairing washers and dryers at night. During the week I worked at a warehouse packaging air conditioner parts with my friend Joe."

"Busy guy."

"I was. I liked being busy and on the go. When I was a teenager, it was like I was supercharged with electricity all the time. If I sat around, I could literally hear the buzzing of cut electrical wire."

"Literally?"

I chuckled nasally. "Yes." I adjusted myself on the couch. "Anyway, I saved up a bunch of money over the summer and bought a whole new wardrobe before school started. I was kind of ZZ Top, you know, 'Every girl crazy for a sharp–dressed man.' I had the sweet–looking car, the baggy clothes, and the attitude. I wrapped my fingers around lit cigarettes and exhaled smoke like James Dean in the movie *Rebel Without a Cause*. Attitude was the key aspect. In the middle of my junior year, I began to break away from being a shy, awkward kid. As time went by, the more confident I became. By the time, school started my senior year, I was ready to kick the door down and claim ownership of the place. I had a renewed determination as well. I wanted to finish high school with straight A's, make a point to the teachers who I felt held me back. I wanted to be popular, a party man to be reckoned with. Get the girls. You know, end in a blaze of glory. It seems funny to look back on this now, but I actually had a list of like ten chicks I wanted to go out with. And down that list I went. If a girl said no, I'd shrug my shoulders and cross her off the list and move on to the next one. During the first month of school, I snagged this blonde girl named Lori West. I think she lasted about a week. She was weird, and kissing her was like a giant bird swallowing your face. Yuck! About a week after I ridded myself of Lori's bad kissing, I met another girl. She wasn't a blonde but captured me in the same way Christine had. I'm not sure why I hadn't noticed her before, but one afternoon in late September, I saw her at swim practice. As soon as I saw her, I knew I had to be with her. She had long, dark brown permed hair and big, brown puppy dog eyes. She was about five-foot-two and moved with a kind of grace. When she walked, it was like a postcard picture portraying a beautiful girl in a white sundress and a wide–brimmed sun hat picking daisies in grassy field on a sunny day. I was mesmerized. I had to fight through a few guys to get her, but I won. After a lot of flirting and playing it cool, I finally got her. When we first started dating, I remember being torn between her and Christine."

"What was this amazing girl's name?"

"Oh—sorry. Her name was Marie."

"Sounds like a French name."

"She was, actually. Maybe that was part of her allure. Anyway, I still thought of Christine in a love–at–first–sight sort of way, but Marie made me feel that way too. I remember being confused for a week or so until I heard the lyrics in a song by the band R.E.M. When I first heard, 'This one goes out to the one I love. This one goes out to the one I've left behind. A simple prop to occupy my time. This one goes out to the one I love' I was driving down Avenue B in my Mustang. When I heard those lyrics, I understood something about life. Sometimes, people in our lives are props, preparing us for a next phase."

"Your eyes were opened to a truth."

"I suppose. At the time, I just knew that it was time to let Christine go and be with Marie. Our relationship was much more than anything I had ever known. When we weren't in school, or I wasn't working at the laundromat, we were together. We played backgammon in her bedroom, we went to movies, we went on long romantic walks on a golf course at the edge of town, and we made out in the car until our lips were numb."

"She sounds like a first love."

"Yes—I would call her that. At that time, my idea of love was infatuation and complete focus. In many ways I lost my self in the relationship. I quit hanging out with my friends or working on my car. I was completely focused on spending every free moment I had, until the end."

Setting my empty mug down on the end table, I quickly scooted forward on the couch and stood up. "Now I've gotta run to the bathroom. Is the bathroom back there?" I asked, while pointing toward the dark area in the back of the cabin.

"Yes. The light switch is on the left side of the door."

"Okay. I'll be right back."

As I walked into the darkness, I was blind until my eyes adjusted. As I moved deeper into the darkness, I could see faint flickers of orange light on the walls. Within each flicker of light, I could see a dark outline on the left side of a short hallway. Beyond it was another dark outline that appeared to be Michael's bedroom in the back. As I reached the dark outline on the left, I turned into it and crossed my right arm over, feeling the cold wall for the light switch. As my fingers moved over a protuberance, I lifted it up. Immediately, a bright light appeared, causing me to see purple splotches in the air.

The bathroom was rustic looking. Directly in front of me was a prominent logwood wall with a four-paned window in the center. The window was bordered with wide wooden planks. Along the logwood wall stood an antique tub with ornamental pedestals. On the left side of the bathroom was a yellowish pinewood lavatory cabinet with a simple water basin in the center. Above the sink was an oval mirror. Next to the lavatory cabinet was a white porcelain toilet. Above the toilet was a double-door, yellowish pinewood cabinet. As I looked down to the floor, I saw a brown oval rug with bears and deer in the center.

I shut the door and relieved myself. When I was finished, I flushed the toilet, opened the door, and switched off the light. As I turned right and walked toward the fireplace, I could see the back of Michael's head in the chair. His white curly hair reflected yellow light. To the left of the fireplace, my shoes were propped up to maximize drying. I hadn't noticed it before, but a smoky, pine-like smell hung in the air. The windows in front of me were black except for reflective flickers of orange-yellow light. When I arrived at the couch, I sat down.

"Much better," I exclaimed.

Michael chortled. "Tea will do that."

"It will," I said, nodding my head in agreement.

"You were about to talk about the end. What happened?"

Michael's question made me feel heavy and weighted down. "As I was saying, I was obsessed with Marie. I couldn't eat, sleep, or drink a glass of water without thinking of her. At the end of the school year she went to stay with her dad in New Hampshire. We wrote each other religiously and sometimes talked on the phone. For the first few weeks, we remained dedicated to each other. But as time moved forward, she drifted away, and I heard from her less and less. When she came home, she acted different. I remember being incredibly excited the day she came home and drove to the airport to meet her. But when she got off the plane, she acted annoyed. She rode home with her parents, and I followed behind them in my car. I thought maybe she was being shy around her parents, but that wasn't it. In fact, when we were finally alone, she turned away from me when I tried to kiss her. At the time, I didn't understand. Looking back, there were so many clues. The day before she left for New Hampshire, she told me that we should date other people over the summer. At the time, I was dumb and didn't understand why she would say that. Later, I would figure out that when someone suggests 'we' see other people, it means they already are. I was just so blind with infatuation that I didn't pick up on the clues. After she came home, she stayed funky for a couple weeks. Of course, her rejection only caused me to become more obsessive and chase her even more. But no matter what I did, there was a weird distance. And then one afternoon she called me and asked if I would come over. I remember the day vividly. We sat together on her parent's blue recliner and talked for a little while. Then she took off a bracelet I had given her and said she wanted to break up. I was devastated! Emotionally it was like a jarring car wreck."

"I'll bet that was hard," Michael said with a sympathetic face.

"My head was definitely spinning. Here's the weird part. When I got into my car to drive home, a song with lyrics 'Love will make you blind' was playing on the radio. How weird is that?"

"Weird or. . . a message."

"Too bad I didn't get that message earlier," I said, wryly.

"Or you weren't listening when you did. If we look, there are constant messages being delivered to us, through people, songs, writings, or events. We just have to listen."

"Yes—that is true. Looking back on things, I received messages along the way."

"What happened after Marie broke up with you?"

"A rogue wave slammed straight into my life, leaving a mess behind."

"Sounds ominous."

"I had a lot of change all at once. Breaking up with Marie was only the beginning. Michael, did you have a first love?" I asked.

A knowing grin appeared on Michael's face and his eyebrows moved upward. "Yes, I married her."

In a teasing voice, I questioned, "You married the first girl that came along?"

"Yes. Much like your stories about Christine or Marie, I fell for Karen when I saw her. You may be too young to remember what a carhop is, but she worked as a carhop at the A&W."

I laughed loudly. "I know what a carhop is. I wasn't born on another planet. A carhop is a waitress that delivered food on roller skates. In the fifties and sixties, drive-up diners were popular, where people drove their cars up to a station and ordered food."

"So, you are familiar with carhops. Well, the first time I met her I was cruising around in my Falcon with friends and pulled into the A&W. I remember thinking that she looked like Grace Slick—the uh, singer for Jefferson Airplane. Do you know who Jefferson Airplane was?"

"Yes. Now you're just insulting me," I said.

"Great group! I saw them play at the Monterey Pop Festival in 1967."

"You were at the Monterey Pop Festival?" I said, admiringly.

"I was. It was a crazy weekend! I remember seeing Jimi Hendrix and the Rolling Stones play. When the Rolling Stones came out, everybody rushed the stage. People were stoned and tripping on acid. That was the first time I'd seen hippies. Toward the end of the show I had to run out when the Hells Angels started fighting with the hippies. It got violent fast."

"Wow! That's pretty cool."

"Back to Karen. I was crazy about her. She had brown hair and blue eyes. I remember when she skated up to the car, she was wearing a short red skirt and a white top."

"Did you take the exhaust pipes off and rev the engine."

"Funny! No—I had my friends in the car, so I played it cool. I went back a few times before she agreed to go out with me. I remember that she wouldn't go out with me alone, so one of her friends had to tag along on our first date. I must have done something right, because we ended up dating throughout high school. She was a grade lower than I was, so I graduated a year before her."

"So that's it? Maniac Michael quit partying for a carhop girl?"

Michael threw his head back and laughed loudly. "Far from it. I got the girl because I was fun. We dragged Main Street on Friday and Saturday nights. We went to parties out at the lake. I was just as wild as I was before I met her. A difference between you and me was that I still went out with my friends. Maybe not because of our choosing, but because of circumstances. Karen came from a poor family and had to work in order to have a car. She was also more responsible and hard-working than I was."

"Odd that she would go out with you then."

"Not really. Girls like wild boys. Otherwise nerds would have the cheerleaders under each arm!"

"True," I said while musing the thought.

"Looking back, more time with friends meant more time for trouble. When Karen was working or doing her own thing, I usually spent my time partying with friends and drag racing. One night, I got blitzed and rolled my Falcon while driving crazy on the country roads."

"How'd that happen?"

"I don't remember a whole lot, but I took a corner too fast and lost control. The last thing I remember was hitting a bank on the side of the road and flipping the car in a field."

"I'll bet your parents were pissed!"

"They were!" Michael nodded his head in agreement. "Whenever I got into trouble, my dad would hand me a rake or a shovel and say, 'Get to work.' I was raking and shoveling around the farm for quite a while." Michael made a digging motion with his arms. "One of my jobs was filling potholes with dirt all the way out to the main road. After a couple months, they felt sorry for me and bought me

151

another car. My second car was a 1964 Mercury Comet. It was cherry—a real nice ride."

"Nice!" I nodded my head, smiling. "It sounds like being a bad boy paid off."

Michael laughed. "I'm not sure about anything paying off. I was the baby of the family and my parents were in their late forties when I was a teenager. By the time I came around, they were too worn out. Rather than deal with my discipline issues, they mostly bailed me out. Being older, my parents were established and had the ability to buy us nice things. What they should have done was make me get a job and save up money for the next car. I never really had consequences for things. So, I continued partying and having a good time. Eventually I blew the motor in the Comet and moved onto another car. I had some nice ones over the years."

"It's your parent's fault that you partied and wrecked cars? They didn't discipline you hard enough." My question wasn't attacking, but I had my own issues to figure out.

"No, bud, that's not what I'm saying at all. We are all responsible for the decisions we make. I made my own decisions. My parents, God bless 'em, loved me dearly and gave me a good life. But it was out of their love and kindness that I never had consequences. They bailed me out because they loved me. I don't blame them for anything. Parents have to trust their instincts and do what is right in their hearts. They can provide all kinds of boundaries, but ultimately kids will choose their own paths, and life will happen just as it's supposed to. You know what I mean?"

I nodded my head silently. Michael's words hit me hard. I thought of my future children and wondered if I would become like Michael's parents or get it right. "Aww, what is that?" I screamed.

"What's what?" Michael asked.

"That blinding light. Man, it's like someone shined a flashlight in my eyes—first my left eye and then my right."

Michael had a confused look on his face. "I don't see any bright lights. Are you okay?"

I rubbed my eyes while they were shut tightly. "Whatever it was, it is passing. I saw this blinding light in each eye for a few seconds and then it stopped."

"Hmm. I wonder if you injured your head more than I thought," Michael said, with a concerned look on his face.

"I feel okay. Up until a few seconds ago, I've felt fine except for that nasty bump on my head." I opened my eyes more fully and sat up straighter, stretching my body on the couch. As I stretched, my body felt achy.

CHAPTER TWENTY-SIX

W hen I looked toward the fireplace, my eyes locked on a center flame. It was brighter in the base and center, yellowish–white in the middle with dark yellow outer edges. The flame bounced up and down as if it were trying to reach the top of the fireplace. I hadn't noticed earlier, but Michael had portraits on the fireplace mantle. I could faintly see pictures of two young boys and a girl. The pictures prompted me to ask Michael about Karen, the girl he married.

"When did you marry Karen?" I asked.

"I'll get to that. I should finish talking about my high school years, so that things make more sense. I wrecked the Falcon during my junior year. The more I got into trouble at school, the more I partied in the car, the more trouble-makers I became friends with. People of a particular likeness escalate others around them. Let me give you some examples. Top athletes such as Olympic teams often push each other toward excellence. Think of the Olympic swimmers

Michael Phelps and Ryan Lochte. Individually they are top athletes who could certainly acquire gold medals without anyone's help. They possess an internal drive to best themselves. But when you put the two of them in a pool, swimming side-by-side, they push each other to greater heights. Because of the competitive push, they not only win gold medals, they break records. They enhance each other beyond their own internal drive. Another, more insane example is a political mob. People start off with idealistic intentions, protesting with peace and thoughtful discourse. As emotions grow, the people push each other to greater emotional heights. Eventually, as we often see, cars become overturned, rocks are hurled at police, and ultimately destructive mayhem takes over the event. The point is, the types of people we surround ourselves with frequently influence our behavior. My party friends pushed me deeper into that life, reaching greater heights like athletes." Michael winked. "I started out drinking a couple of beers and stopping there. But with harder–partying friends I was encouraged to drink more. 'Hey, pansy! A six-pack is all you can handle!' We pushed each other to drink harder. As the group grew, other types of members came into the circle, escalating to grass and speed. In the middle of my senior year, a friend and I robbed a gas station in a neighboring town."

"You robbed a gas station? Like put face masks on and pointed a pistol at someone?" I said, astounded by his revelation.

"No. We broke in late at night and mostly stole cigarettes and beer."

"That's crazy! Did you get caught?"

"Yes, and later the police figured out it was us. We were dumbass kids who left clues behind."

"So, what happened? Did you go to jail?"

"I was arrested and went to jail for part of a day. My parents bailed me out, and later I went to court. I was put on probation, and my parents had to pay a pretty big fine. At the end of my senior year, my dad pushed me into the navy. I remember him saying, 'Maybe the military will straighten your ass out!' In the summer, I left the farm and Karen behind and went to boot camp."

"Your dad basically sent you to war for robbing a gas station!"

"I don't think that was his intention. I think he wanted to get me away from Sagebrush and mature through military discipline. He wouldn't have made me go to Viet Nam. He probably didn't think that far ahead. My parents were mad, and I didn't have other prospects. I spent most of high school in detention, and my report cards were below average. My family had the means for college, but I was too wild and had friends to cruise the country roads with."

"When did you marry Karen?" I asked, my curiosity growing.

"After boot camp I went back to Sagebrush in the late fall while on leave before my first tour of sea duty." Michael became sheepish. "While I was on leave Karen and I got engaged. We married quickly in late December."

"Wait, I thought Karen was a grade lower than you."

"She was. She was a senior in high school. After we got married, she came out to San Francisco and finished high school."

"No way! That's freakishly similar to a woman I know. She married her first husband while she was a senior in high school."

Sidestepping my comment, Michael continued, "Bud, all of our lives have intersecting points with others. Think of a large grid of dots and lines connecting them in straight and diagonal lines."

I looked upwards while I mused Michael's grid concept. "I don't disagree with what you are saying. In fact, my sister and I have often talked about that. When we were kids, we lived in south Denver, near a Catholic school. It was only two blocks away and we used to ride our bikes around there. Neither of us attended school there, but I actually played that school in soccer, baseball, and basketball. Well, her future husband went to that Catholic school and was only a grade behind me. It is highly likely that my sister and brother-in-law crossed paths at some point, each unaware of the future."

"Exactly, bud. Exactly," Michael said, nodding in agreement. "You left off with your breakup with Marie and a tidal wave of change, I believe."

"Right. I'm feeling dehydrated. Can I get a glass of water?"

"Absolutely." Michael got up from his chair and walked over to the kitchen. I heard a cabinet creak open and a few seconds later water running. When the water turned off, I could hear Michael's heavy boots on the floor. When he reached the couch, he lowered a glass of water in front of my face.

"Thanks." I grabbed the glass of cold water and took a long drink. As the water moistened my mouth and throat, I felt relieved. The inside of my body felt dried and parched, like a sun–burnt desert. I lowered the glass and exhaled a satisfied "Ahh!"

As Michael was sitting back into his chair, he asked, "How is your head? Any more flashes of light?"

"No, that was brief and went away fast. I admit that I feel a little achy but okay. Thanks for the water by the way."

"No problem."

CHAPTER TWENTY-SEVEN

I began to remember an afternoon when I was heading home from Arizona Southwestern College out on the edge of Sierra Vista.

In my mind's eye I could see the interior of my Mustang. It was light blue with white, black, and blue tiger–striped fur seat covers. My steering wheel was covered by a black leather cover that I had fastened with vinyl braids. The instrument panel was rectangular with a wood looking plastic panel. A large tachometer was directly behind the left side of the steering wheel, a large speedometer directly behind the right side. On the left side were smaller gauges, a battery gauge on the top, and a temperature gauge on the bottom. On the right side was a smaller oil pressure gauge on the top with the fuel gauge below it. As I looked forward, I could see the teal hood scoop and the gray asphalt and white line on the left side quickly passing by. All around the car was empty desert and a sky turning orange from the afternoon sun. "Wind of Change" by Scorpions was playing on the radio. I remember feeling empty inside, as if life had been pulled from within me. No joy, no sadness, no belonging, just emptiness. I desperately wanted to talk to my friends, but many of them had either gone off to college or the military. Marie had moved on to a new boyfriend. I had nowhere to go, except home where everything was in chaos. I remember how the lyrics "The wind of change blows straight into the face of time, like a storm wind that will ring the freedom bell" tugged at my emotions. I felt a sense of irony within my life at that moment. Everything did feel like time was blowing, sending me rolling like a tumbleweed. Funny how a song captures a moment in your life.

"When Marie and I broke up, I was like a lost puppy who couldn't find his home. Most of my friends went off to universities or the military while I stayed in town attending Arizona Western College. We broke up about two weeks before the semester started, so I was struggling with loss and change at the same time. During my senior year of high school, my dad's drinking was totally out of control. It was bad—really bad! He would get drunk and sit on top of the house ranting and raving, or he would ride around town on his bicycle, brown bagging a forty in his hand. When he started doing crazy shit like burning his arms with cigarettes, my mom kicked him out. During the last few months of my senior year, he stayed with one of his drinking buddies who lived outside of town. Things kind of continued to spiral downwards over the summer until my mom decided she'd had enough with all of it. We held several garage sales to get rid of stuff, and my mom moved the rest of what we had to Denver. My sister, Tommy, and I were still in school, so we had to stay with our grandparents for a couple of months. In December that year, we drove to Denver in my car. That was my first road trip. Anyway, all of this hit when I broke up with Marie and started college. It was like I was in a hurricane's vortex for months."

"That's a lot of change at once," Michael said quietly.

"I didn't realize it at the time, but breaking up with Marie was kind of a blessing. Otherwise, I would have stayed in Sierra Vista. Had I stayed in town for Marie, I would have dropped out of college to work and support myself. Knowing how everything turned out, things had to happen as they did."

"Yes, they did. Often, we kick up against circumstances in our lives, but in many cases, we are pushed in certain directions for a reason."

"My sister and I arrived in Denver on Christmas. I remember that the streets were covered with snow, and it was super cold. I had never driven in the snow, and neither of us owned winter coats. While driving to my aunt's house, I slid through a four–way stop and landed in someone's front yard. I remember putting the car in reverse and spinning my back tires like crazy trying to get out. I imagine I trashed someone's lawn."

"Probably did! You didn't do it on purpose though. Did you leave a note or anything?"

"No, I was too frazzled and tired from driving all day. When I got back into the street, I drove super cautiously to my aunt's house."

Michael smiled. "You should have been driving cautiously in the beginning."

"Nineteen–year–old boys are rarely cautious."

"What happens next, Bambi? I'm assuming you learned to drive in the snow."

"I did. I even learned to fly down the streets at forty miles an hour fishtailing."

Michael looked toward the outside windows and then

looked at me. He smiled and waved his hand in a circular motion. "What happens next?"

"Well we lived with my aunt and uncle for a couple of weeks until my mom found a place. By the grace of God, she found a job a few weeks after she arrived in Denver. While she waited for my sister and me to arrive in Denver, she and Tommy stayed with my aunt, saving up money.

"My dad eventually checked himself into a VA drug and alcohol treatment center. As I recall, he stayed in the facility for about six weeks. Later he told me it was a lock–down facility, and he had to ask very nicely to do anything." I laughed. "Honestly, I think he disliked following the rules." As I spoke to Michael, I vividly remembered driving down Sixth Avenue one frigid night and being miserably cold.

It was frigidly cold, and my teeth chattered as I drove. For some reason there was hardly any traffic and I had all three lanes to myself. The night was foggy, and my face was illuminated by the green glow of my dash lights.

"When I think about our move back to Denver, I remember being cold all the time—that's what I remember."

Michael ignored my comment. "Did treatment help him?"

"Not really. I remember he came to live with us in the new place for about two months until he started drinking and sneaking off to who knows where. Later in the spring he moved to a low rent apartment in south Denver. Things got kind of crazy. He frequently partied with the local alcoholics and got mixed up with drug dealers."

Michael was silent for a while. "What about you? What were you up to?"

"I was lost the first few months. In early January I tried to get into school but missed the deadlines. Plus, I was an out–of–state resident and couldn't afford tuition. That meant I had to hang out for a year. Sitting around the house was driving me nuts, so I started looking for jobs right away. About three weeks after we moved to Denver I started working at a restaurant as a bus boy. I hated that job, so I quit and went to work nights at a gas station in a rough part of north Denver. I'm surprised I didn't get killed. I saw a guy carjack a woman's car and drive off with her baby in the back. One never forgets the blood–curdling scream of a woman chasing after her baby. And then there was the transvestite guy who liked to stop by and masturbate in front of the windows. I'm not sure why, but I stayed at that job through the summer though." I lifted my hand up. "Don't ask me why. I think as long as I was making money, I'd put up with all kinds of things."

"You were driven. The means are just a way to the end."

"I suppose. I've never thought about it like that. But yes, I would say that I am an achiever for sure." I looked down and realized I was still holding an empty glass in my lap. I reached over to the end table and set the glass down. "Anyway, this period of time gets funky. I didn't have any friends in Denver, so I looked up some kids I went to elementary school and junior high with. They had become total partiers and smoked pot all the time. I fell in with those kids, smoking weed and drinking quite a bit. Somehow in the mix of that my perspective and goals changed. My college major was business and computer science, and over the course of that year, it became psychology. That's what pot does for you!"

"Again, things happened for a reason. Those kids would have been kids you went to high school with had you not moved to Sierra Vista. You were meant for something bigger —not sitting around passing the bong back and forth."

I laughed out loud. "I suppose, Michael. At the time I was heartbroken over Marie and felt like my life was upside down. I couldn't find any normalcy. My dad's substance abuse continued to escalate. While I worked at the gas station, he frequently came to the gas station late at night with weird people, asking me to cash suspicious checks. Thankfully at the end of the summer, this construction guy started hounding me about working with him. I remember how forceful he was. He'd call me up and say stuff like, 'Do you want to get shot?' After being pestered for a couple weeks, I quit my job and started working with him. I'm glad I did though. It ended up being a cool job where I learned a lot about home improvement and acquired skills that would serve me well later."

"Yes, that was a good opportunity that came along."

"Hey, I want to hear about Karen."

CHAPTER TWENTY-EIGHT

"Yes, I need to explain more about my life. As I was saying earlier, Karen transferred to a high school in San Francisco. I was on ship duty at that time and out to sea for months at a time. In the summer Karen gave birth to our son. He was born with health issues. I've always blamed those crazy ass injections and chemicals the military sprayed everywhere."

"Did you sue or fight the government?" I inquired.

"Hell, no! We were a couple of kids who didn't have money or know any lawyers. But at least the navy paid for his medical bills. I was stationed in San Francisco for a year, and then I was transferred to San Diego. We never lived on base. In fact, houses were cheap back then, so Karen and I bought our first house in Chula Vista."

"Wow! You never hear cheap and San Diego in the same sentence anymore. You should have stayed. You'd be rich by now!"

Nodding his head and smiling, Michael said, "Yeah."

"Well, it all worked out. You became a family man and settled down, right?"

"No, far from it. I was a troublemaker, just like I was in high school. I partied all the time when I was on shore leave. When I drank, I did crazy things. One time I rode around on my motorcycle with my son on the gas tank doing wheelies and speeding around the neighborhood. All kinds of things could have gone wrong, but I swear that kid had a halo of light around him. When I was away at sea, I clowned around on the ship, getting into trouble. In fact, I was demoted at one point for doing handstands on a ship tower."

"What? That's crazy! Wasn't there a war going on?

"Ah, a two–edged question. Why wasn't I busy looking out for the enemy, and who the hell gets demoted during war time? I did! My life in high school continued into the military and my marriage. The navy kept me stationed in San Diego for four years. When Karen became pregnant with our daughter, I got out of the navy, and we moved back to our home town in Colorado."

"Sagebrush?"

"Yes. I worked a lot of odd jobs until I started driving a truck. For a few years I was on the road driving cross country."

"It's like you were in the navy. Rather than at sea, you were at the highway."

"I haven't ever thought of it that way, but yes. During those years, my partying escalated. While driving a truck I drank in bars and took black beauties to stay awake while driving. I—"

"Black beauties?"

"Black beauties are speed."

"Didn't know that."

"As I was saying, when I was home, I fell back into my old life. I partied in cars, putting one in a ditch and rolling the other."

"So, your dad didn't change anything by sending you off to the military."

"No. I will get to this later, but no matter what my dad did, my life was going to fall into its own destiny. Our lives have things in them for a reason."

"Okay—so what about Karen? Did she party with you?"

"No. Karen was like she was in high school. Mature and hard-working. She took care of our children and kept the house going."

"She put up with that? Sitting at home with kids while you partied like a rock star."

Michael laughed. His hazel eyes rounded and his cheekbones became prominent. "Hell, no! We had many, many fights. She threatened to leave me several times. As this went on, my parents and a bunch of other people convinced me to quit driving a truck and move out of Sagebrush. Again, I was pushed to leave my party friends behind and move to another place. In this case, Denver."

"Did things change?

"As they say, wherever you go, there you are. No, I didn't change. I found new friends who drank and used drugs. The only thing moving to Denver changed were my drugs of choice. I discovered cocaine and much more trouble. I worked for a series of car dealerships, and we eventually lost our house out on the edge of Denver. We moved to a house in south Denver near the Platte River."

I wondered about Sophia's patience. "Karen must have been a rock, raising two kids while this went on. You're a lucky guy, Michael. Not many women would stick around for that—at least I don't know any."

"Karen *was* an amazing woman. Her life had purpose and a path separate from mine. Her path was raising the kids who in turn had a special purpose in life. I was an orbiting satellite of chaos, but her life had meaning too."

"Wow! Your story gives me a lot to think about."

"We're not done, bud. Tell me, did you finish college?"

"Wait, wait—hold up," I said, extending my right arm up with my palm facing Michael. "Are you telling me you were just a back-seat passenger to life and it all just happens around you?"

"No, absolutely not. We all have choices. Yes—I had a predisposition for alcohol and drugs and made choices that involved them. That was my challenge to overcome. Deep down I wanted to change. But in the end, not even Karen's threats of leaving compelled me to make better decisions. I would have had to humble myself and change everything to overcome my addictions."

"Are you saying we choose to do destructive things?"

"No. You're missing the point." Michael said defensively. "Tell me more about college. Did you finish?"

CHAPTER TWENTY-NINE

Sighing, I rubbed my forehead and face with my right hand. "I don't understand your point. What does my life story have to do with you?" I asked, betraying frustration in my voice.

"You'll see. Just humor me," Michael said, in a quiet but passionate sounding voice.

"Okay—well, as I was saying I had to wait a year before starting school. The following spring, after we moved to Denver, I enrolled at Red Rocks Community College in Lakewood. I quit my job with the contractor and went back to the gas station, working nights three days a week."

"You went back to that dangerous gas station?"

"Yes. I needed a job, and the gas station was quick and easy. I had worked my way up to assistant manager before I left, so I had a good reputation for working hard. Anyway, I worked and went to school. I didn't drop my party friends right away. In fact, I continued hanging around them for a few semesters of college."

"You followed in your dad's footsteps?"

"No, not really. The difference between he and I was that I never really enjoyed that life. Drugs made me stupid, and I hated being dysfunctional. Eventually I became sick of hanging out with morons and got serious about school and my future."

"You are driven, and people around you didn't slow you down."

"Yes, I suppose. I think a lot of things came into play. My dad's life intersected with mine a lot. I saw him homeless. He attempted suicide a few times, and he was in and out of facilities like the Salvation Army. He was a constant reminder of how things can become. Plus, over time I got over Marie and started to feel happy again."

"Did you meet any girls in college?"

"A few. Most of them were never serious. I went out with a blonde girl named Jessica a few times. She was kind of punk and changed her hair color every few weeks. One week she would be strawberry blonde and the next have bright blue hair. It was like going out with a wild–haired troll doll. After her, I met my fiancée, Sophia. She was so cute. A guy at work said I couldn't get her—and well, I never let something go unchallenged." I chortled and leaned back into the couch. "But I wasn't ready for her at the time. I was too busy chasing the weirdest girls I could find."

"What does that mean?"

"It means I went on some weird dates. I remember this girl named Debbie who told me she wanted to sleep with one hundred people. At the time I thought she was joking. That's nasty—and it was only our first date." I laughed out loud.

Michael laughed. "Well. . . some have a different kind of path."

My body convulsed in a cringe. "Ick. I guess. Anyway, I

kind of pushed through college, getting the best grades I could. Similar to high school I had a crazy desire to finish with all A's one semester."

"Did you?"

"Yes—just like high school, I finished with all A's. . . I guess I kind of left this out, but while I was in college, I left the gas station and got on with a good company, working my way up the ladder. When I graduated from college, I stayed working with them, moving through a series of jobs."

"Why am I not surprised that you worked in college?"

"I guess I haven't talked a lot about her, but my mom was always a catalyst, suggesting ideas and pushing me— ouch!" As I was speaking to Michael, I felt a sharp stabbing pain in my left arm.

"Are you okay?" Michael said, with a concerned look on his face.

"I don't know. I just felt a stabbing pain in my arm."

"What can I do to help?"

"Nothing. I'll be fine."

Michael gruntingly said, "It's getting a little late, but I'll throw one more log on," as he heaved himself out of his chair. He reached into the box on the right side of the fire-place and produced a log. As he set the log into the fire, sparks flew out from the bottom. He grabbed the metal poker rod and moved the bottom logs around.

As Michael moved the logs, the flames became more alive, wrapping around the new log. The flames looked as if they were arms grabbing onto the log and pulling it down-ward. I wondered if that was what hell was like. Flames grabbing hold of us and pulling us deeper into the consuming fire, left in ashes.

"You said your mom was a catalyst? How so?"

"My mom was always hard working and the responsible

one. She kept our house going. If it wasn't for her, I don't think we would have had food or roofs over our head. While I was growing up, she pushed me toward sports, academics, and later jobs and career paths."

"She controlled your life?"

"No, not at all. From time to time, she would suggest things that would later alter my path for the better. I was driven to do things on my own, but my mom sort of nudged me in certain directions. Later I would figure out that when I didn't listen to her, things didn't exactly work out that great. Originally, I was a computer science major in college and this would have served me well later. Instead, I chose to smoke weed and become a psychology major. While I acquired some useful people skills, the computer classes have propelled my career a lot faster. It all worked out, but the road could have been easier. Anyway, she was a catalyst that guided me toward a good career and stuff. I'm glad I had her because on the opposite side I had my dad's chaos to contend with. During my junior year of college, he met this crazy woman who was just as obnoxious as he was. They both compulsively drank, floated in and out of hotels along Colfax Avenue and jail. From time to time he visited me when I was a cash–strapped college kid needing money."

"Did you give him money?"

"You know, I've always been generous. If someone needs help, I will help them. I was hard working, but I wasn't selfish about money. My dad's life was difficult to watch, but he was still my dad. I honored my parents no matter what."

"I'm sure he hated asking you for money and was always grateful," Michael said, with slight smile. His eyes sparkled.

"I guess. It probably had more to do with the fact that my mom dragged all of us to church every Sunday. I had as much positive influence as I had bad. Sometimes I think it was meant for me to know both sides of life for some reason. I sometimes see things in a wider perspective than others. As I mentioned earlier in the evening, I was always on the outside looking in. That was true for my family life as well."

"Hitting fast forward, what happened after college?"

"I continued working for the same employer I had in college and lived in a rundown apartment complex until I paid off my student loans. Then I moved to an apartment in the mountains near Golden. I loved it up there."

Michael turned his head and looked toward the windows again. He looked as if he were waiting for something to happen. I couldn't figure out why he looked toward the darkened windows. Maybe he was concerned about the snow.

As he turned his head back toward me, Michael said, "I imagine there was an intersection at some point—whose path did you cross?"

Michael's comment struck me as odd. "Well, yes, I did cross someone's path—Sophia's."

"Tell me about that."

"I will in a minute. But first tell me about your life in south Denver." I gestured and imitated his expression in an attempt to tease him.

Michael laughed loudly. "Smart ass!"

CHAPTER THIRTY

"When we moved to the house in south Denver, I continued in my downward spiral, getting lost in drugs and alcohol. Rather than spending time with my family, I was out partying like a single guy. I went to jail a few times and couldn't hold jobs. As I sank deeper and deeper into my addictions, my marriage continued to spiral downward, and I ruined friendships."

I interrupted Michael, "That's what I don't get. Why didn't Karen tell you to cart your ass down the road? I know I would have!"

"I doubt you would. Responsible, hard-working people tend to take care of other people around them. Karen's path was to be the caretaker. I pushed her life's trajectory, just as others pushed mine, or people have pushed yours."

"I'm not sure if I believe that, but go on," I said, waving my hand impatiently like Michael.

"I knew my life was a mess. I didn't need anyone telling me that. I just couldn't turn things around." Michael straightened in his chair and flashed a knowing smile. "The truth is, I was caught in a vicious cycle, where I drank to forget my problems, which in turn created more problems to drink about. I couldn't cope with life because I never learned any coping skills. So, I kept drinking."

"You sound like a Bloody Mary advertisement."

Michael laughed. "Yes—I needed a drink to cope with my hangover. Exactly." Michael's smile faded to a look of seriousness. "The downward spiral eventually led to a suicide attempt when I could no longer face my problems and believed others would be better off without me."

I thought of the day I dragged my dad out of the garage. "Suicide is never an answer. It's a selfish act and hurts everyone around you. It doesn't make their life better."

"You're right—it doesn't. At the time, I was too lost in my problems to see that. I was sorry for the hurt I caused everyone, but never knew how to say it." He paused as if he wanted to say something. "Bud, I was sorry for a lot of things, especially my suicide attempt."

"I'm sure you were."

"After that event, I went to that town you lived in—Sierra Vista and stayed with my brother."

"No way! That's weird you lived there too."

"All paths intersect at some point." Michael scratched the back of his head, ruffling his white hair. "My brother convinced me to seek treatment and get my life straightened out. It would be the first of many attempts."

"How long did it take you to get your life turned around?"

"I never did. I stayed clean and sober for a while. I even joined the Catholic church." Michael winked at me and smiled broadly. "I got a good paying job and convinced Karen to start over. After a few months, she finally agreed, moving herself and the kids to Sierra Vista." With a look of disappointment, he continued, "But I fell back into my old life and eventually, I found new friends who used meth and cocaine. My drinking continued to escalate until I lost my job and Karen kicked me out again."

As Michael spoke, there was something familiar about this story. Strangely we lived in the same places and lived similar lives, though in different periods of time. As I thought about Michael's strange familiarity, he continued to talk.

"When Karen kicked me out, she was at the end of the road with me. I went to stay at a friend's place out on the edge of town, but I just made a bigger mess of things. Karen finally gave up and moved back to Denver and lived near her family."

Wait a minute! I thought. *How could this be?*

"James, the reason I wanted to share our life stories is to show you something." Michael nervously looked at the dark windows again. The yellow firelight pulsed up and down, casting dark stretching shadows. "The day I took my first drink with friends in high school, I put my life on a trajectory. Just as you put your life on a trajectory when you were a teenager. You chased goals, and I chased booze!"

"I didn't chase goals," I protested.

"You made choices to accomplish things, set goals for yourself and reached them. Whether the goals were something as simple as attempting to bench press more weight each week or as lofty as finishing college with straight A's; you continually sought to raise the bar. And no one around you distracted you from that. Not high school friends, not Marie, not the pot smokers, not anybody."

"You make it sound as if I consciously chose all of that."

"You did and you didn't. Within you, you had a drive, almost like a survival instinct. My point is that everyone's lives are a narrative, like a story in a book. There are things and people along the timeline, but there is a common theme. The same was true for my life. From a young age, I found trouble. Maybe if my parents had been stricter and given me less opportunity for trouble, I would have avoided a life of substance abuse. I doubt it though. That first drink was enough for me. Maybe I wouldn't have wrecked my own car, but instead rode with a friend who crashed us both and wound up dead."

"You don't think that if your parents had curbed your behavior more, you would have lived a normal life?"

"No. After spending a few months in this cabin, I've realized that my narrative was about choices and overcoming my own obstacles. No one could have done that for me."

"All night, you have said that our lives intersect for a reason and things happen as they should. Are you telling me that drug addicts are meant to be?"

Michael raised an open palm toward me. "No—that's not what I'm saying. I had a strong drive toward pleasure seeking and avoiding internal feelings such as fear. Alcohol felt good and made me less fearful. Just as your drive to accomplish goals is more about your desire to control outcomes. You never had control of your life in any other aspect, did you?"

"That's crazy!" I said, exhaling powerfully.

"Is it? Isn't the reason you don't want children is because you are trying to control an outcome. You're an achiever wanting to be an ideal parent and fearful of the elements you can't control."

"No, I don't."

"James, avoiding the future because you fear the unknown is more about control than anything else. Within your fear of children, you are attempting to grasp control of an outcome. If God gives us free will and choice. What makes you think you can decide for everyone around you when God doesn't? Isn't that what you are trying to do in your relationship with Sophia?"

"What the f—" I said, jumping up from the couch. "Who are you? How could you know that? I've never shared that with anyone, not even Sophia." I remembered seeing the pictures of two boys and girl on the fireplace mantel. I stalked toward the fireplace to look at them. As I grew closer, I realized who they were. The pictures were of my sister, Tommy, and me.

"We're almost out of time, bud."

As I turned around and faced Michael, I hurled a series of rapid–fire questions. "Running out of time for what? Who are you? Where did you come from? What are you doing here? Is this all real, or am I dreaming this?" Was I in some kind of time warp? My mind reeled while I tried to grasp the conversation with Michael.

Without answering me, Michael continued, "James, you have a gift. As you said, you have always been on the outside, watching others as an observer. This was never meant to be a punishment. You see the narratives. You see your own, you saw mine, and you see Sophia's. I'm sure it drives you nuts to imagine your children with narratives that may include trouble and hard times, but their narrative will happen as it needs to. All you can do is be is an example for them and show them an alternative life."

"I'm trying. I struggle because I don't want them to end up like my Dad or Tommy. What if they chose friends who are on a bad path, seeking pleasure and escape? What if they are super smart like you were but fall into the same kind of life."

"They might. You have no way of knowing that. You can see the narratives, but don't know the end of the story."

"Then how is that a gift and not a curse? I can see the narratives but have to simply watch them?" I remembered a recent news event where a teenager with mental problems shot up a high school, killing nearly twenty kids. As the news reported on the kid's life and how he had a history of mental issues and struggles in school, I remembered being annoyed and wondering why people didn't see the kid's path and try to alter it. The kid lived in foster care, owning a bunch of weapons and no one thought to take the guns away so that no one would be harmed. What if he chose to commit suicide rather than shooting dozens of people? Either way, everyone around that kid should have seen the future.

"You can reveal to others what you see and let them decide. That's what life is—it's a series of choices. Earlier I spoke about life being like a bunch of dots in the sky connected by lines. The lines represent our choices and movement to other dots or points in time. They are also our clues that we made a bad choice or a good choice. People always blame God when bad things happen. God gives us free choice. When bad things happen, it is because someone around us made a bad choice. If he controlled everything, our lives would be nothing more than scripted narratives."

"I guess that makes sense."

"I was given an opportunity to bring you to this cabin and help you see the narratives. We began our stories in Sierra Vista because that was an intersection point. You made choices that moved your narrative forward to where it is today. I made choices that fatefully ended mine."

My head was pounding, I could feel my heart racing.

Dad. . . is that you? How is this possible?

Michael put both of his hands on the chair's arm rests and pushed himself up into a standing position. He grabbed the iron poker on the side of the fireplace and pushed the remaining log backwards, rolling it to the back of the fireplace. All that was left were dark red embers faintly glowing red. On top of them were caps of black and gray. Turning toward me, he said, "Goodbye, Jamie!" Then I watched him turn and walk into the darkness, out of my sight.

Suddenly everything went out of focus and started spinning out of control. The cabin became jumbled like I was looking at it through a kaleidoscope. "Dad!" I screamed. My head was pounding, and my body ached.

Then there was nothing but black.

CHAPTER THIRTY-ONE

"His heart rate is 120 beats per minute! Pupils are reactive to light!"

My eyelids felt heavy as I struggled to lift them. I felt cold and my body ached painfully. Each time a loud siren penetrated my ears, my head felt dizzy and thick. As I struggled to lift my lids, I saw a blurry white ceiling with a man and woman hovering over me and yelling.

"Blood pressure is one-sixty over ninety! Temperature is ninety-six point five degrees!"

My body jostled left and right. Thinking of a flickering flame, I fell into dreamless sleep.

CHAPTER THIRTY-TWO

As my eyes fluttered open, I saw a white ceiling with bright, square florescent lights above me. Daylight filled the room. As I looked to my left, I noticed a tube running into my arm from a bag filled with liquid. I felt dreamy and confused. Inhaling deeply through my nose, I turned my head to the right. As I looked to the right, I saw Sophia sitting in a chair, head down, hands folded in prayer.

Sensing I was looking at her, Sophia quickly jumped up and moved closer to the side of the bed. "You're awake. You have been mumbling for hours and screaming for your dad. Oh, James, I have been so worried!"

"What happened? Where am I?" I asked weakly.

As she forced a smile, I could see concern and worry written across her face. Her eyes were red and swollen. I could tell she had been crying. "Darling, you were in a bad car accident." Softly caressing my right hand, Sophia said, "We nearly lost you yesterday. I was so scared! I couldn't bear the thought of losing you. Thank God you are awake."

Groggily shaking off the fatigue I replied, "The last

thing I remember was driving down Colorado Boulevard. I faintly remember I was on my way to Breckenridge."

"Someone in an SUV pulled out in front of your car and you slammed into the side of it. You never made it to Breckenridge. The police estimated you were going fifty miles per hour and said that you didn't even have time to hit your brakes."

"How long have I been here?"

"Three days. They had to keep you sedated while the swelling in your head came down. Yesterday your heart stopped! They didn't think you were going to make it, but I guess God has other plans for you!" She took my hand in hers and gently caressed it. "I don't know what I would do without you!"

As Sophia told me about the accident and being sedated for three days, vague memories of a white–haired man smiling at me in a dark cabin with orange firelight swirled in my mind. My head painfully felt like it was being crushed in a bench vise. I felt groggy and my mind was hazy. Was it all a dream or was it real? The man with white hair didn't look like my dad but seemed like him. I didn't go to Breckenridge? As my mind came back to the conversation with Sophia, I heard her voice.

"You will need at least eight weeks to recover. How are you feeling?"

"My head is pounding, my body is sore, and I feel foggy —out of time. It's hard to explain."

"It will take a while for the sedatives to wear off. They say seven days for each hour you are under, or something like that."

Sophia's seriousness made me chuckle inside. As my mind came into greater focus, I immediately thought of my Mustang. "Is my car totaled?"

Shaking her head, Sophia rolled her eyes and half-smiled in derision. "You nearly died and have broken bones —and all you can think of is your Mustang?"

I shrugged my shoulders. "I loved my Mustang," I said with a sheepish smile.

"Well, we love you and are thankful you came back to us. It is only by the grace of God a nurse was checking on you when your heart stopped! Otherwise you wouldn't have survived!" A tear slid down the side of Sophia's face as she lovingly gazed down at me. "Your mom should be here soon. She and Jack are driving up from the Springs."

As I looked at Sophia's beautiful face, I felt comforted. Sensing I should lighten the mood, I joked, "So I get to go pick out a new Mustang."

"Oy! You don't need a fast car. And besides, I'm never letting you out of my sight again."

"But how will I bring you flowers?"

"Pick them in the yard."

"And if it's winter?"

"Draw me a picture of them."

While we both chuckled, A doctor wearing a white lab coat abruptly walked into the room. He was tall and slim with short black hair. He had deep-set eyes and thin red lips.

Quickly grabbing a chart hanging at the end of the bed, he said, "I am Doctor Levy. How are we feeling today?"

"Tired and my chest hurts," I replied.

"Well, you have a broken collarbone, three broken ribs, and a cracked sternum. You will be very sore for a while. On a scale of one to ten with ten being the most excruciating pain you have ever felt, how much pain are you in?"

"I don't know. Eleven."

"Okay, I'll have a nurse bring you something." Lifting

the top sheet on the clipboard, he quickly scanned the next page. "Blood work is good. If we continue to see a reduction of swelling in your head, we should be able to send you home in the next couple of days. Once the swelling clears, I will order another scan to be sure there are no residual concerns," Doctor Levy stated in a monotone voice.

As her eyebrows lifted and her face revealed a look of surprise, Sophia inquired, "So soon?"

"James has a mild concussion. Previous scans did not reveal any fractures or hemorrhaging. If he continues to improve, he should be able to continue recovery at home. "

"Are there instructions for us to follow?" Sophia asked.

"We will give you instructions for home care and will set up follow–up appointments. Because of the head trauma, you will need to watch James for signs of depression, dizziness, nausea, vomiting, slurred speech, loss of consciousness, or motor loss. We will need to see him right away if he has these types of issues. Otherwise, it is fine for him to recover at home. There are numbers to call if you have questions. James will need rest and time. No strenuous activity, but doing light activities such as walking will be okay."

"Thank you, Doctor Levy. I would prefer to recover at home. How long do you think I'll be off work?" I asked.

"As I mentioned to Sophia, with the type of fractures you sustained, your recovery will take approximately six to eight weeks. You will have a loss of mobility while your arm is in a sling. I'll get you a note for your employer," Dr. Levy rattled off.

"Okay," I replied.

"Do either of you have any other questions? I'll have the nurses inform me as soon as the swelling visibly subsides."

"No, we do not have any questions right now," Sophia replied.

As I watched Doctor Levy make notes on the clipboard and hang it back on the bed, I thought of the dream. Narratives and cycles. Then I thought of Sophia wanting kids.

"James, wait here, I want to talk with Doctor Levy," Sophia said, walking behind Doctor Levy.

Snickering, I teased, "Where would I go?"

Continuing to walk toward the door with her back to me, Sophia replied with a deeper voice, "You're a pain in the butt!"

While a smile lingered on my face, I let my head sink back into the pillow and I closed my eyes.

"And you will know the truth, and the truth will set you free."
John 8:32

CHAPTER THIRTY-THREE

The healing process was slow, but after three months I began to feel better, and strength in my right arm was returning. It was a constant struggle navigating life with my dominant arm in a sling. My left hand was completely useless. Relationships at work had been strained but were slowly improving. I think my boss was tired of my excuses for missed emails. In my defense, I wasn't able to efficiently use the computer and struggled to click on email messages with my left hand. That white–haired overseer had no idea how impossible it was to uselessly grip the mouse with my left hand and clumsily navigate the computer. I felt like an awkward eighteen–month–old baby holding a spoon and directing food toward my mouth.

Sophia and I decided to delay the wedding until mid-May when the weather was nice. We were worried about the typical spring storms in March and April. Plus, my arm wasn't quite one hundred percent yet.

I settled with the insurance company and bought a new

Mustang, despite Sophia's many protests and threats of abandonment.

Following the accident, I was often preoccupied with the vivid dreams I had while unconscious. I had a sense of several days passing. Michael didn't physically look like my dad yet seemed so much like him. Only my dad called me *bud*. How did Michael know that? I wondered if he was my dad visiting me from heaven and my mind manifested Michael's image in the dream. I recalled the night I sensed a spirit in my backyard. Was there a connection?

The conversation with Michael Morris left me thinking about my childhood, my dad, and my grandparents. Michael was right and my life has been full of patterns and life events occurring in intervals. I graduated from high school exactly twenty years after my dad and graduated college, exactly ten years after junior high. My grandpa was in the first graduating class of his high school. My dad was in the last graduating class of his high school. I was in the first graduating class of a high school. Three generations, alternating first and last. I'm not sure what the patterns meant or why I noticed them. I tended to think they were signs giving me a glimpse of understanding. Perhaps life is not as random as we think. Maybe life is pre-planned, and I'm just along for the ride.

The more connections I sought out, the more I found. Starting as a little kid, I traveled to California every ten years. As an adult I have traveled to Hawaii on ten–year intervals. By sheer happenstance of a car accident, Sophia and I will be married in the same month, ten years after my mom's second marriage. The connections and strange patterns continued to coalesce.

Michael was right, events did seem to be connected on an invisible grid. Perhaps life events are points on a grid, and our choices move us in points on an axis in various directions. Yet, it's a grid that is specific and unique to each one of us. I can choose when and where to go to school, but I don't perceive the choice to be a neurosurgeon because it's not on the grid. Rather, I choose between an IT profession or a teaching profession because they are points on my unique grid.

Over the past three months my thoughts went in circles, linking seemingly divergent events or things together. I even had the crazy notion of my cars being linked. I'm sure I would have been fitted for a straitjacket if I shared these thoughts with anyone. I thought I was nuts, and surely others would have thought so too.

There were many similarities between Michael Morris and my dad George Fisher. Like Michael, my dad was raised on a farm and moved back and forth between California and Colorado. In high school he was constantly in trouble, and my grandfather pushed him into the military during the Viet Nam era. Like Michael, my dad also fell into a life-long pattern of substance abuse and lived a very dysfunctional life. The conversation with Michael was like an interwoven tapestry of time and events, linking my life and my dad's life. I would be lying to myself if I didn't admit the dreams impacted my view of parenting someday. I had a sense of destiny.

Breaking free of my thoughts, I walked into the kitchen and switched on the overhead light. I loaded water and coffee grounds in the coffee pot and waited for it to percolate. I absentmindedly watched steam puff from the top while I wait for the carafe to fill.

When the percolation ended, I reached into the cabinet, grabbed a cup, and filled it to the brim with hot coffee.

In my mind's eye, I could see a flickering flame. There

was a yellow band bending and twisting around a darker center with a hue of blue shining underneath. I thought about the fading dream where I talked to Michael and drifted to memories of my dad and his disordered life. I thought about his teenage years racing down country roads with a beer in his lap and wrecking cars. I imagined his repentance and promises to my grandparents to get his act together. I remembered stories of their forgiveness and replacing everything that was lost, stolen, or broken in his life. I envisioned the periods of a perfect son and then cycles repeated with new calamities. My whole childhood and adult years were filled with chaos, calamities, repentance, forgiveness, and dreamy calm followed by a new and improved version of chaos. I turned inward to my mind's warehouse of file drawers, opening and closing memory drawers searching for something to give me insight. Thinking of my grandparents, I tried to channel their decisions and what they might have done differently. While I thought about my grandparents I drifted to my life. A part of the reason I struggled with the idea of raising children was because I long ago lost the connection to my teenage self. When chaos hit, I either got on my bike and rode far away from it or turned to weightlifting to vent my anger. While I later dabbled with drugs in college, I never found solace in them. Instead I threw myself into whatever work I had, frequently channeling myself through college papers I considered works of art. Even though I struggled to remember my teenage feelings, I knew that my future kids, like all other kids, would have struggles of their own. *What if I'm an asshole and don't even know it?* What if I raised kids in a home that was the opposite of mine, and yet they fell into the same life my dad lived? What could I do to change the family patterns? I hated the feeling of helplessness.

Wrestling with my thoughts, I got ready for church.

"For as Jonah was three days and three nights in the belly of a whale, so will the son of man be three days and three nights in the heart of the earth. . ." The priest read from the Gospel of Matthew.

I listened with intent focus.

Sunday mass at St. Elizabeth's was inspiring and uplifting. When we exited the doors, the springtime smells caused me to be mentally transported to my elementary school days. I instantly recalled playing around the swings during morning recess, buzzing with as much energy as spring itself. I remembered the pleasure of lying face down on the warm sand heating my chest and stomach when the morning air was still crisp, but warm enough for the teachers to send us outside without jackets.

Excited birds chirped loudly while Sophia and I stood outside with Doug and Katherine Thompson, our marriage prep sponsors. The late morning air was still a little crisp but warming as the sun moved overhead.

Katherine and Doug were empty-nesters: They were an older couple with three raised children who had left home. Doug was a tall, thin, mustached man with a mostly receded hairline. What hair he had left was the color of salt and pepper. Katherine was short, with intertwined blonde–gray hair that was shoulder length and curly. Presently, she was wearing an orange–red dress that highlighted the lipstick on her thin lips.

"Let's meet at the Corner Bakery," Sophia said with an animated voice.

"Sure—that sounds good," Katherine said. Turning toward her husband with a playful backhand on his stomach, "How about you, Doug—that sound good?"

"Yes, that sounds fine, hon," Doug affirmed.

"Where's the nearest one?" I asked.

Doug pointed west. "Uh—there's one off of 16th Street mall—down by California Street."

That would be too far for all of us to walk. "Should we just meet over there?" I asked. A resounding and unanimous "Yes" set our group in motion.

Looking around, I noticed the Corner Bakery's décor had a woodsy ambience. The walls were covered with dark wood about halfway up from the floor. The front counter was dark wood, and all the tables were dark wood as well. The large menus hanging on the wall above the front counter were dark as well.

Hushed voices mixed together as patrons sat at tables conversing with each other.

The four of us silently stood in line, eyeing the menu, not out of awkwardness but indecisive focus. "I'll pay for all of these!" I yelled from the back of our group's line. My offer resulted in turned heads and refusals to let me pay, but I batted them all away. "It's on me Doug—that's final!"

After we received our locator flags, we stopped at the beverage station on our way to a table near the window. Each of us chose the black currant tea.

When we sat down at the table, I could see mountain peaks reaching over the houses and trees in the distance. My heart warmed with the realization that spring was upon us and the further we sojourned into it, the more colorful

Denver would become. It was a long winter, way beyond calamities in the weather and temperature variations.

"So how is work going?" Doug asked.

"It's going okay. I've been really bogged down with meetings lately. Management wants to move our systems to something called the cloud. Definitions for it are all over the place. Personally, it sounds like a rebadge of what we already have, a shared services center."

"I hear that word at my work." He chuckled. "Of course, I'm an old school architect who prefers a drafting table over a computer, so I don't pay too much attention to it. They can put the computer into outer space for all I care."

Doug and I both laughed. When silence followed, I noticed Sophia and Katherine were turned to each other, intently talking about something. Ignoring them, I turned back to Doug, filling in the silence with small talk. "Ready for golf this year?"

"You bet. I already entered into a big tournament in June. I have a fifteen handicap, so I need to get out there and practice." He paused for moment. "You should come play sometime," he said while slapping me on the shoulder.

"Me? No—I suck at it. Besides, it's kind of an expensive sport."

"The course we play at isn't too bad. Really depends on where you go."

I politely nodded. Truth be told, I hated golf and found it boring. I'd much rather race the golf carts across the grassy hills. While Doug droned on about golf, my mind wandered to thoughts of Michael and the possibility of our lives having patterns and moving along on a grid.

When my mind came back into focus, I blurted out,

"Do you think there are patterns within our lives—or circumstances guide our decisions?"

In the abrupt silence, Sophia shot me a knowing look, Doug appeared to be rudely interrupted, and Katherine stared at me with a blank look on her face.

Initially Doug fumbled for words. "Uh-uh—sure, James. I've noticed many patterns in my life. In fact, Katherine crossed my path a few times before I asked her out. I believe the Lord puts signs in our life to guide us in the right direction, sure."

Katherine chimed in. "That's right. If we look closely, we see signs to guide our decisions. Over the years I have come to believe that when we feel remorse or agitated while making a decision, it's the Holy Spirit speaking to our hearts, guiding us."

Sophia's face continued to hold a knowing smirk. "James, do you remember when we talked about the dream you had, and I told you it sounded like the story of Jonah and the whale? When we heard the gospel today, I wondered if you were thinking about that."

"But how do we know?" I asked.

Doug continued, "The bible is full of examples, pointing to generational patterns and connections, mostly through numerology. The ancient Jews wandered in the desert for forty years. Jesus spent forty days in the desert and after his resurrection, Jesus spent forty days with his disciples. I read in a commentary once that forty is the symbol of transformation."

With an excited voice, Katherine interjected, "Yes, and there were twelve tribes led by Moses, and Jesus had twelve disciples. The book of Kings narrates twelve cycles of sin and repentance."

Husband and wife seemed to tag team each other. Doug

quickly followed. "The bible shows us many patterns and circumstances to show us that God has a plan for us. Think about the story of Jesus' birth. Mary and Joseph couldn't find a room in an inn and wound up in a barnyard stable away from town. And it just so happened that if they stayed in an inn, that may have been discovered by King Herod who wanted all first-born dead. . . circumstances guided their safety, even when they didn't understand it at the time."

As I was about to respond, a young waitress with short black hair approached our table.

With a high–pitched voice, the waitress asked, "Chopped Caesar?"

"Right here," Katherine replied.

"The southwest salad?"

"That's mine," Sophia said.

"Chicken Pomodori?"

Doug silently raised his hand.

"And the uptown turkey avocado?" Bouncing on her heels and displaying a chipper looking face, the waitress continued, "Can I get you anything else?"

Sophia, Doug, and Katherine smiled and shook their heads.

I said, "No, I think we're good."

"Okay—enjoy!" The happy waitress spun on her heels and walked back to the front counter.

While I looked down at my turkey sandwich, I pulled the toothpicks from each half cut diagonally. Before I picked up a sandwich half, I smashed it down to reduce the height, as I knew it wouldn't fit in my mouth. *Alligators must eat here*, I thought. "A while back Sophia pointed out a bible verse that talks about stumbling by disobeying the word. . . as is their destiny. Do you think that is true?"

Sophia silently stirred the salad with her fork, coating everything with citrus–ranch dressing,

Doug said, "Why sure, James. That sounds kind of like the parable of the sower's seed."

"Oh, I remember that story. It's about God planting seeds."

Doug chuckled. "Well, it tells a deeper story than growing vegetables. The parable shows us that the soil represents our disobedient lives. Some fell on the path and the birds ate it up—sounds like sin around us. Some fell on rocky ground where growth sprang up in shallow soil, and when the sun rose it was withered because the roots were not deep—sounds like our inability to stay on the path of righteousness. Some fell in a thicket of thorns, and where it grew, the thorns choked it—sounds like sinful people we keep around us. But some seed fell on rich soil, and it produced fruit thirty, sixty, one-hundredfold. That sounds like obedience to God's plans."

Katherine turned her head in astonishment. "Doug, that was truly enlightening. I may need to reread that one."

Doug sat up straighter and tilted his head with a broad smile. "Well, thank you, honey. It just sort of came to me just now." Doug chortled, appearing to be surprised by himself.

"I don't know if I've ever thought about it like that." I pondered the thought. "There's so much more meaning behind bible stories than I realized." I felt like such a dolt when it came to the meaning of the bible. I had heard that parable in church many times and never realized we are the soil.

"Amen to that," Doug said.

"Circumstances might help us along, but in the end *we* choose. The bible can show us the mysterious ways the Lord works, but it's up to us to open our eyes, ears, and hearts, and let God's will guide us," Katherine said.

Maybe they were right. Patterns ebb and flow in our lives, serving as lighted guideposts. Maybe I was allowed to see the destruction of addiction all around me so that I might make changes.

Changing the subject, Katherine inquired, "The retreat is coming up—are you two ready?"

"Yes," Sophia and I said simultaneously.

"Doug and I will be praying for you."

"Thank you," I said.

With that, we moved into the business of marriage preparation and counseling: what to expect and what to prepare for. Marriage prep seemed tedious, but it was designed around the right intentions. After all, we would be standing before God promising an oath of faithfulness to each other. If you can't do the time, don't do the crime, as they say.

CHAPTER THIRTY-FOUR

The three–day retreat was held at a secluded house south of Larkspur. The house was nestled in a valley surrounded by mountainous terrain and pine trees that purified the crisp air with their pleasant scents.

Over the weekend, couples huddled in a tight–quartered living room space while an older couple navigated course materials, spotted with life experience and testimonials. I counted knots in the log beams above us during a few of them. Every few hours, the couples were sent outside to discuss supplied questions with each other.

Sophia and I were attentive and responsive to the guided questions. However, an unspoken and unacknowledged tension remained between us throughout the break–out sessions. Sophia was waiting for something; I could sense it but never addressed it.

At night we were separated, men to their bunk beds and women to theirs. It was the worst two nights of sleep I ever had. Not only because of the loud snoring and uncomfortable bunk bed, but also because of our unspoken tension.

CHAPTER THIRTY-FIVE

Two weeks from the wedding, I went to a park near my house in south Denver. While I sat in the grass overlooking a steep hill covered with green grass, freckled with yellow dandelions, I mused over the one thing Sophia wanted.

It was a bright, sunny day with a cloudless, blue sky stretching overhead. Trees within the park were full of leaves: the ones caught in the sun's rays were light green, and the others were dark green. The electricity of springtime filled the air while birds loudly chirped, squirrels ran from tree to tree, and children's voices bellowed from a nearby playground. Everyone was bursting with energy, even me, though mine was more of a nervous kind. Deep within my soul, I loved Sophia, but two weeks before a wedding, one wonders, no matter how great thy love.

I thought about my grandparents who were meticulously organized and clean. They worked hard to provide a typical 1950s household and like most people of the time avoided emotionally charged conversations or outbursts. Things were the way they were, and you either sank or you swam. My grandparents were strict but also gave generously to my dad and his siblings. My dad was never without or in need.

Yet deep within my dad, an inner emotional current ebbed and flowed, often fueling an intense desire to drink and self-medicate with illicit drugs. The threat of losing his family, job, money, cars, or life never stopped him. In the end, the only thing that stopped his substance abuse was death itself.

Similar to my dad, my maternal grandpa's alcoholism followed the same path. There were lost jobs, lost money, and bouts of anger. Yet, he never stopped. Not because he was heartless and immoral, but because the addiction wouldn't let him. From the moment of his first drink, it latched on to his ankles and never let go.

I couldn't speak for my sister or Tommy, but growing up poor and in constant emotional turmoil generated an intense desire to spurn my dad's circus life at all costs. While I was like most twenty-year-old kids of my generation and dabbled in substances, I predominantly threw myself into studies and worked hard to avoid being poor and dysfunctional like my dad. I pursued my career with enthusiasm and purposeful drive. Inwardly I had a strong predilection for self-improvement and constant perfection. From an early age, I seemed to have a point of view that other's around me didn't have. Somehow, God was guiding me, that much I knew.

While reclined in the grass with my hands propped behind me, I could feel the sun's rays against my face, warming my skin. A gentle breeze occasionally wiped the heat from my face. I inhaled deeply, delighting in the air smelling of fresh linen.

I realized that nothing in the universe is random, and for every one thing, there is an opposite. There is positive and negative, matter and anti-matter, light and dark, life and death, good and evil, and even the simplistic right and left. Even the solar system has oppositional balance with four solid planets and four gaseous planets orbiting the sun. Nevertheless, I contemplated opposites and the ordered universe. I wondered if it was so throughout the generations.

I questioned if there was truth behind biblical scriptures such as the book of Exodus where it stated, "The Lord, a merciful and gracious God, slow to anger and rich in kindness for a thousand generations, and forgiving wickedness, crime and sin, yet not declaring the guilty guiltless, but punishing the children and grandchildren to the third and fourth generation for their fathers' wickedness." Or in the book of Ezekiel, where it stated, "If a man begets a son who, seeing all the sins his father commits yet fears and does not imitate them. . . this one shall not die for the sins of the father, but shall surely live." Did our ancestors succumb to temptations and sin with generations to follow suffering the temptations of their forefathers because of sin? Did it take the strength and will of a particular generation to change the fate of the family line? If this were true, then my inner strength and will may be the saving grace that changes our family. Maybe God had been guiding, illuminating my vision, and my children would be okay after all.

The story of Adam and Eve wasn't solely about an apple and a tree or the admonishment of a woman. It's a figurative story describing the original disobedience and how that disobedience destroyed a family, sending evil decisions down the line. Later, that family's dichotomy was revealed in the story of Cain and Abel. Cain chose the path of malicious evil and Abel chose the path of goodness and offerings to God from his heart. Two sons, one father, two totally different choices. Did parenting affect the outcome?

Scholars frequently debate nature and nurture. Some scholars argue that nature is the more powerful genetic force that overrides learned behavior through automatic predisposition. Other scholars argue that nurture is an even more powerful force, where learned behavior overrides genetic tendencies. Nature scholars often cite stories where a kid is raised in the perfect environment yet develops along genetic lines. Conversely, nurture scholars cite stories such as the inner-city kid who was raised in abuse and poverty during his formative years and later turned around by the strict but caring coach at the neighborhood recreation center who guided him away from the cycle of abuse and poverty.

By the time I got up and left the park, a lightbulb seemed to come on in my head and illuminate my thoughts. Perhaps everyone has their own path in life, each filled with struggles, triumphs, happiness, love, and sadness. My child's life may be a struggle with addiction, and mine had been a struggle watching others around me destroy their lives. Maybe life isn't about what happens during our lifetime. Maybe life is about what we learn and how we improve. But I have to believe that it is as Christ described to his accusers when he performed a miracle on the Sabbath. *The son does as he sees the father do.* What if I became the generation–changing example, showing my son by what I do?

Getting into my Mustang and driving home, I realized that God wanted me to learn and experience things. It was never about how I lived; it was about what I learned. In my dad, I saw the end. In my marriage and future children, maybe I would witness the beginning.

In the grand scheme of the universe, it all turned out the way God planned. My grandparents did the best they could, my dad did the best he could, I would do the best I could, and one day, my children would follow.

CHAPTER THIRTY-SIX

"Early this morning a family of five were fatally crushed when a bridge collapsed while their car passed underneath," said the news reporter.

As sunlight shone through the bedroom windows, I awoke to the local news blaring on the TV. I must have fallen asleep watching *Star Trek* reruns. As I groggily looked around, I felt jittery inside like I was about to bungee jump off the edge of a 2000–foot suspension bridge. Our wedding was tomorrow. I had a million things to get done. I needed to pick up my tuxedo, get my hair cut, wash the car, and get a manicure. I wasn't sure why men get manicures when they get married, but everyone said I had to do it.

Sophia and I were to leave for Maui right after the wedding. I was looking forward to ten days of sunbathing, swimming in the blue ocean, and fresh seafood.

I rolled onto my back and blankly stared at the white ceiling sliced with light and dark shadows. While my mind came into focus, I remembered a summer day during my childhood.

The water was cold to the touch as I slowly moved my hand back and forth while I lay face-down on the edge of my inflatable boat. I could see my reflection in the murky water as the sun's rays turned its color from dark green to a bright mossy green.

I loved my boat and rowed it all over the channels that snaked between the houses set off from the lake. Occasionally, boats caused gentle wakes as they journeyed to their docks. But not in that moment. In that moment, the water was as clear as glass while I lay on the edge watching snapper turtles climb on a floating platform called "Turtle Town." The platform artfully held a stunning replica of old–west buildings that looked like a scene from the O.K. Corral.

Grandpa affectionately named my boat the dingy. It was blue on the bottom and yellow on the top with blue and yellow oars. I rowed that boat all over the place. One day an old man yelled, "Kid, don't you get tired rowing that boat?" When I yelled, "No, sir!" he laughed heartily, seeming to enjoy my youthfulness.

It was another lazy, sun–filled day in June of 1983. The air smelled tangy and fruity. In the corner of my eye, I could see Grandpa picking cherries from the tree adjacent to their blueish–green colored house. On the other side of the house stood a giant weeping willow that shaded the covered dual-slip dock.

Earlier that morning, Grandma scolded Jennifer and me for lying in the guest house watching reruns of *The Bionic Woman*, *The Six Million Dollar Man*, and the *The Hulk* for too long. "It's a beautiful day outside, and you two are wasting it" was still ringing in my ears.

On some mornings, Jennifer and I ran to the dock, screaming, "Claudia, Claudia," until a lanky thirteen–year–old girl appeared in the bushes across the channel from us. But not that morning.

Other days, I fished for bluegill and catfish off the edge of the dock or vigorously rowed my boat exploring the channels, imagining I was a sailor explorer discovering strange and new lands like a character from *Treasure Island*. But not that day.

As I lay, face down in my boat watching the turtles in calm water on that lazy afternoon, I was mesmerized.

The summer I spent at the lake with my grandparents was the happiest summer of my life. I loved that dingy; I rowed that boat everywhere. I remember when school started in the fall, I had arms of steel. Not a boy on the playground could beat me arm wrestling.

I think what I missed most over the years was the simplicity of my days being on the water. Some days I was bored but a good kind of bored, the kind of bored a kid experiences when they have no deadlines, no complications, no stress, and no responsibility. The only thing was deciding if I wanted to row my boat, fish, hang out with Claudia, or watch reruns on TV until I pissed my grandmother off.

I rolled out of bed and walked into the kitchen to make some coffee.

Maybe my kids would be addicts of some sort. Heck, most kids are addicted to video games in our modern era, and society seems to accept that. Either way, something will come up and it will be unexpected.

As I thought of the lake, I felt a stirring in my heart. I loved kids, and I really did want to be a father. I think the Holy Spirit had been prodding and sending me messages all along the way. Had I just been too narrowly focused on my point of view and ignoring what everyone had been telling me?

I thought of the story of the man who kept crying out to God to save him from the raging flood waters while he was stuck on his roof. He was fervently praying when a rowboat came by and a man shouted, "Jump in, I'll save you!" The man on the roof stood firm, resolutely saying, "No, no, I have prayed to God, and he's going to save me!" The man in the boat shook his head and rowed on. A while later a motorboat came by, and the driver said, "Hey, jump in—I'll save you from the floodwaters!" The man on the roof shouted, "No thank you! I'm trusting that God will answer my prayers and save me!" The motorboat went on. When the man was up to his neck in floodwaters, a helicopter flew overhead and upon seeing him hovered. The pilot shouted down, "Quick, grab hold of the line, and I'll hoist you up!" The man on the roof yelled, "No, I have faith in God—He'll save me!" The helicopter flew on, looking for survivors. The floodwaters eventually overtook the man, and he drowned. When the man arrived in heaven, he ran toward God exclaiming, "I prayed and had faith you would save me, but you failed me! Why did you forsake me, Lord?" God replied to the man, "I sent you a rowboat, a motorboat, and a helicopter. What more did you want?"

I thought of Bunk, Thelma, and Michael. Bunk told me not to focus on the negative things in life. Thelma said that it wasn't for us to judge other people's lives. Michael showed me that our lives are a narrative where each of us makes choices, and we cannot control what may or may not happen.

I'd been that idiot on the roof this whole time! I quickly picked up my phone and dialed Sophia's number. I could hear the phone ringing in my ear.

"Hello."

"Hey, it's James."

"Oh—good morning."

"So how many kids should we have—two, three. . ."

EPILOGUE

I must have paced the hotel room one hundred times the morning of our wedding, racked with nervous energy. I couldn't sit still and even worse, I fumbled with my bow tie until the photographer arrived to snap pre-wedding photos. We were supposed to take a photo of me dressing in my tux and gazing out the window in anticipation. I gazed out the window, all right. In between the pacing, I frequently stopped to peek out the windows and breathe in the spectacular view of the mountains surrounding Breckenridge.

I'm not sure why I was so nervous. I loved Sophia to the moon and back. I couldn't imagine my life without her. I chalked my nervousness up to the fact that I was about to stand in front of our family and friends reciting vows. What if I fumbled the words? What if I got emotional and embarrassed myself? What if I said the wrong name? I thought of that *Friends* episode where Ross says Rachel's name while he is marrying Emily. I laughed to myself when I thought of Ross's friends coming up to him saying, "*Emily*—not

Rachel!" While pacing, I told myself I must be sure to say *Sophia.*

After the photographer tied my bow tie and the photo was finished, I left the hotel and headed over to St. Mary's. As I drove up, I noticed the church's nineteenth–century style architecture. It was white with a steep gabled roof and bell tower. The stained–glass windows were Gothic looking, and a simple white picket fence corralled lush green grass.

The church was modern on the inside. The altar was raised with three steps surrounding its half–moon shaped edge. The pews were light–oak colored and arranged angularly versus in a straight line. The walls were painted white and a large stained–glass window hung behind the altar. A large crucifix hung to the left of the altar.

I stood in the narthex for a few minutes before a frantic woman who appeared to be in her early sixties hurried toward me saying, "You can't be here! You and the groomsman need to wait downstairs." I nervously complied and ambled down a wooden stairway that creaked loudly with each step.

After a few minutes of waiting, the church coordinator came down and said it was time for the viewing. I followed her upstairs and stood inside the nave, facing the altar as directed. Behind me was a glass wall between the nave and narthex. I anxiously stood in my spot for what felt like an eternity until the wedding coordinator arrived and instructed me to turn around.

There she was. Sophia was dressed in a simple but elegant wedding gown. Her black hair was pulled up into a bun with corkscrew strands of hair hanging down. Her puppy dog brown eyes met my gaze, and we stared into each other's eyes for a timeless moment. She seemed as self-conscious and nervous as I was. As I stood in front of the window, enamored by her beauty, I could see my own reflection in the glass. My brown hair was neatly parted to the side, my bow tie was crooked, and my blue eyes revealed my nervousness. Our day had arrived. Sophia's and my moment abruptly ended when the wedding coordinator said, "Okay—let's get back downstairs."

When I arrived downstairs, Dave, Pete, and Justin were waiting for me. Pete was my best man. Dave and Justin were my groomsmen. They smiled broadly as I walked toward them.

"You ready to end your freedom?" Pete asked while slapping me on the back.

Dave threw an arm around me and said, "Looking good, brother. I am so happy for you!"

"It's not too late to run," Justin teased. He smiled and put his hands on my shoulders and squeezed.

"No way—Sophia is the best thing that's ever happened to me!"

"She's the only thing that's ever happened to you," Justin joked.

"Yeah, you're kind of a dork, maybe you should hurry up and marry her," Dave said.

The guys and I jostled, poked, and prodded each other until the moment arrived. The moment of truth. In all honesty, I was so nervous that I wanted to hurry up and get it over with. I was not looking forward to standing in front of two hundred people.

The groomsmen and I walked single file to the altar and assembled in our designated positions. Shortly after the men were assembled, "Bridal Chorus" began to play, and the entire congregation stood facing the narthex of the church. I was so nervous my hands became sweaty.

First, Michelle ceremoniously walked down the aisle wearing a red dress and carrying a bouquet of turquoise colored flowers, followed by Michelle was Carrie. After Carrie, Heidi slowly walked to the altar. As Michelle, Carrie, and Heidi arrived at the altar and stood in their designated positions, the music shifted into "Ave Maria." A breathless moment passed before Sophia entered the nave with her father at her side. As she walked toward me, I felt light-headed in the realization that our day had arrived. My eyes focused on her, and one of the things I feared happened. I became choked up inside and tears welled in my eyes, not because I was losing my freedom, but because I was embarking upon a new and wonderful journey with an amazing woman. As Sophia and her dad approached the altar, I walked forward, and he passed her arm to me. When our arms intertwined, I could feel Sophia's warmth against me while we walked to the altar.

Sophia and I chose traditional readings for the mass with the most memorable being Corinthians 13. Love is patient, love is kind. . . seemed to be a fitting reminder for two people embarking upon a lifelong journey together. They would become the words guiding our lives as future storms raged in our lives. The mass was a beautiful infusion of God in our marriage.

After the mass was over, the wedding party and our parents stayed behind for a photo while the guests journeyed a short distance to Terrace Gardens for the reception. We must have posed for fifty different pictures. I was thankful when the photos concluded and we caravanned to the reception.

As we arrived at Terrace Gardens, I was pleased with the festive decorations and overall ambiance. The reception was more than I expected. The DJ announced our arrival as we entered a large, logwood styled ballroom. Strands of yellow lights zigzagged across the ceiling. There were large round tables with white tablecloths and white chairs. On each table were centerpieces featuring a vase with red and turquoise roses and a cylinder–shaped candle wrapped with a gold band. Loosely thrown red rose petals freckled the tables.

When everyone was seated, waitstaff served filet mignon with green beans, salad, and dinner rolls. Sophia and I opted to serve everyone a complimentary glass of wine. The bridesmaids and groomsmen provided entertaining and sometimes comical toasts while everyone ate their dinner. After dinner we partook in all the ceremonial traditions.

When the time came for Sophia to share our first dance, we held each other closely, hugging and occasionally pecking each other on the lips. As I held her in my arms, I felt a sense of joy and belonging.

Gazing into my eyes, Sophia whispered, "I love you always!"

"Always, my love!" I kissed her tenderly and drew her into a tight embrace. The music never stopped, at least not for me in that timeless moment.

ABOUT THE AUTHOR

CA Kirkham lives in Colorado and enjoys spending time outdoors with his family. In his spare time, he indulges in science fiction and mystery novels.

Inspiration for his book derived from addiction within his own family. While on a faith journey, he sought to answer his own questions about addiction, exploring them through the lens of Scripture. As is so often true, the Holy Spirit speaks to us when we listen.

CA Kirkham has led a successful career in information technology, but could never squash the desire to write or to satisfy every English teacher who told him he should be a writer. He endeavors to create stories that inspire readers to ask more questions and explore the deeper meanings of life.